DRACULA

HAMILTON DEANE &
JOHN L. BALDERSTON

DRACULA

THE ULTIMATE, ILLUSTRATED EDITION OF THE WORLD-FAMOUS VAMPIRE PLAY

Edited and Annotated by
David J. Skal

ST. MARTIN'S PRESS
New York

Designed by Visual Cortex Ltd.
Composition by The Sarabande Press

Deane, Hamilton.
Dracula : the ultimate, illustrated edition of the world-famous
vampire play / Hamilton Deane, John L. Balderston ; compiled and
edited by David J. Skal.
p.   cm.
British and Broadway stage adaptations of the play by Hamilton
Deane and John Balderston from the novel Dracula by Bram Stoker.
ISBN 0-312-09278-4 (hc)
ISBN 0-312-09279-2 (pbk.)
1. Dracula, Count (Fictitious character)—Drama.   2. Vampires-
-Drama.   I. Balderston, John L. (John Lloyd), 1889–1954.   II. Skal,
David J.   III. Stoker, Bram, 1847–1912.   Dracula.   IV. Title.
PS3507.E168D7   1993
812'.52—dc20   92-44421   CIP

First edition: May 1993
10 9 8 7 6 5 4 3 2 1

"Yet who would have thought the
old man to have had so
much blood in him?"

Lady Macbeth

Introduction

ALTHOUGH DRACULA IS BEST-KNOWN TO THE PUBLIC AS A QUINT-
essential Hollywood icon, and secondarily as the fictional creation
of the Victorian novelist Bram Stoker, our modern image of the
king of vampires is largely a creation of the legitimate theatre.

Stoker's 1897 novel *Dracula* introduced a Transylvanian vampire almost unrecognizable to generations of film audiences raised
on the familiar Bela Lugosi image. Stoker, too, would have a
difficult time recognizing Lugosi's characterization as having much
to do with his own conception of Dracula. He imagined a 500-
year-old warlord, a cadaverous old man with white hair, a droop-
ing Genghis Khan moustache, bad breath and hair in his palms. In
Stoker's book, Dracula grew younger as he drank blood, but he
never became really attractive. The sexual magnetism, like the
impeccable evening clothes and manners to match, were all de-
vices added to make *Dracula* viable in the theatre. To work within
the conventions of a drawing-room mystery melodrama, Dracula
needed to be a character one would plausibly ask into one's
drawing room in the first place — not a man-beast whose idea of a
social call was smashing through a bedroom window, unan-
nounced, in the form of a slavering wolf.

Still, Bram Stoker was not without a sense of the book's
theatrical values. By the time of *Dracula*'s publication he had
served as the business manager of the Lyceum Theatre for
seventeen years, and as the right-hand man and confidante of the
great Victorian actor Sir Henry Irving. Stoker was thoroughly
steeped in every aspect of stagecraft, but never wrote directly for
the stage (he did, however, write popular fiction voluminously). At
some point it occurred to Stoker that Dracula might be an ideal
part for Sir Henry himself; whether or not Irving "inspired" the

*Opposite: Bela Lugosi in an
atmospheric publicity portrait
for the 1929 stage tour of
Deane and Balderston's
Dracula.*

character initially is a matter of conjecture, although several biographers and historians have commented on the mesmeric, controlling influence the charismatic Irving had over his inner circle.

According to Chicago drama critic Frederick Donaghey, who made the writer's acquaintance during one of the Lyceum's American tours at the turn of the century, "When the late Bram Stoker told me that he had put endless hours in trying to persuade Henry Irving to have a play made from *Dracula* and to act in it, he added that he had nothing in mind save the box office. 'If,' he explained, 'I am able to afford to have my name on the book, the Governor certainly can afford, with business bad, to have his name on the play. But he laughs at me whenever I talk about it; and then we have to go out and raise money to put on something in which the public has no interest.'"

Stoker went on to tell Donaghey his conception of Irving as the king of vampires: "The Governor as Dracula would be the Governor in a composite of so many of the parts in which he has been liked — Matthias in *The Bells*, Shylock, Mephistopheles, Peter the Great, the bad fellow in *The Lyons Mail*, Louis XI, and ever so many others, including Iachimo in *Cymbeline*. But he just laughs at me!"

Sir Henry Irving, near the end of his life, in a portrait by Bernard Partridge. Stoker created the Dracula persona with Irving in mind, but the actor had no interest in playing the vampire on stage.

Despite the high literary pretensions that can be inferred from such comparisons, Donaghey believed that Stoker had few illusions about *Dracula* as a piece of writing. "He knew he had written, in *Dracula*, a shilling shocker, however successful a one, and was frank about it," Donaghey recalled in 1928.

Stoker nonetheless arranged an elaborate staged reading of *Dracula* at the Lyceum on the morning of May 18, 1897. Little is known about this marathon event — it was ostensibly to protect the novel's theatrical copyright — except for what can be surmised from the surviving programme and "script." A cut-and-paste abridgement of the published text was fully cast with talent drawn primarily from the second tier of Lyceum actors. Henry Irving would have no part of it, of course. Dracula was portrayed by a "Mr. Jones," whose precise identity remains obscure. The most

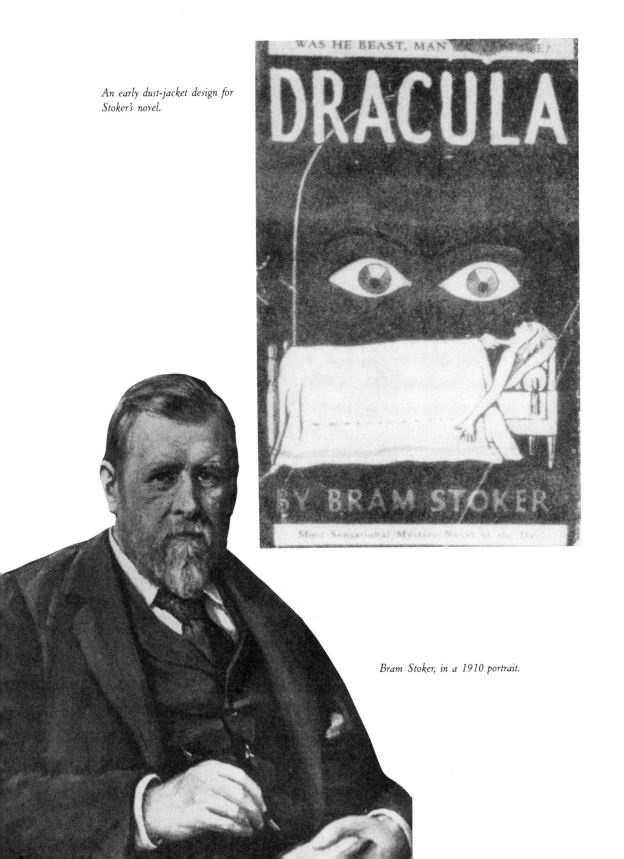

An early dust-jacket design for Stoker's novel.

Bram Stoker, in a 1910 portrait.

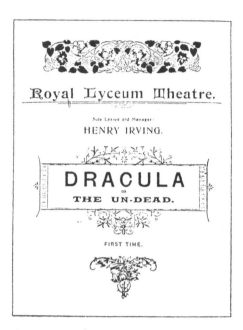

Whitworth Jones was likely the first actor to read the part of Dracula on stage. Below left: Jones made an imposing Fortinbras in Hamlet at the Lyceum (1897); below right, as an Egyptian villain opposite Alla Nazimova in Bella Donna (1912). Jones also acted under the name Robert Whitworth. (The Billy Rose Theatre Collection, The New York Public Library at Lincoln Center, Astor, Lenox and Tilden Foundations)

Program cover for Bram Stoker's 1897 copyright reading.

Edith Craig, daughter of Henry Irving's leading lady Ellen Terry, was the first actress to take the role of Mina in Stoker's 1897 reading at the Lyceum.

reasonable candidate for the part is Whitworth Jones, who the same year portrayed Fortinbras in Johnston Forbes-Robertson's celebrated production of *Hamlet* at the Lyceum — and, judging from an engraving, the very image of Stoker's vampire warlord. (Jones, who also used the name Robert Whitworth, was sufficiently Henry Irving-like to land the part of Mephistopheles in America some years later, and was frequently cast "bigger-than-life" in roles that included wizards, kings, and demons.) Jonathan Harker was played by an actor named Herbert Passmore, and Van Helsing by Tom Reynolds, a popular character actor in Irving's employ.

As the number of speaking parts exceeded the number of characters whose letters and journals formed the novel, it is plain that the event went beyond a mere reading of the text, and had to have been at least semi-dramatized. The Lyceum's musical director, Meredith Ball, received a credit, suggesting at least an overture or entr'acte accompaniment. The reading employed twenty separate settings in forty-seven scenes; whether or not Stoker employed existing set pieces and props from the Lyceum's considerable store is not known. Stoker biographer Harry Ludlam reported that one of the paying customers was Maria Mitchell, the writer's devoted cook.

Florence Stoker, the real-life "Bride of Dracula" who jealously guarded the dramatic rights to her husband's masterpiece.

Following Stoker's death, his widow Florence (née Balcombe, a Victorian beauty in the Pre-Raphaelite mode and the youthful adoration of Oscar Wilde) was left with few tangible assets, save her husband's copyrights, and the only one that continued to generate income was *Dracula*. Forced into genteel poverty, she clung to the demon jealously. Florence also found security in Catholicism, to which she converted in 1904, eight years before her husband's death. She had been attracted by the pomp and theatricality of the Catholic ritual as it was practiced at the Brompton Oratory, one of the most sumptuous Catholic churches in England. The degree to which she found a resonance between the blood-drinking of the mass and the similar preoccupation of her husband's creation is not known. Nonetheless, Dracula became Florence's guardian angel, of sorts, providing a steady, if meager sustenance. She was determined to make money from stage and motion picture rights, but interlopers vexed her. A now-obscure film called *Drakula*, made in Hungary by director Karoly Lajthay in 1920, seems to have escaped her notice. But when *Dracula* was pirated by German filmmakers in 1921, Florence launched an international campaign against F.W. Murnau's now-classic *Nosferatu: A Symphony of Horror*, and, armed with a judgement in her favor by the German courts, very nearly destroyed all existing prints. Fortunately, the film and its negative survived in scattered fragments; reconstituted, it was eventually recognized as a classic of the German cinema. Harry Clarke, the celebrated illustrator of Poe, wanted to produce an edition deluxe of *Dracula* incorporating his creepy, Beardsley-like ink drawings. The widow didn't like the terms proposed by Clarke's agent, and book collectors were thus denied a macabre masterpiece.

Opposite: First published in 1897, Stoker's Dracula *has virtually never been out of print. Here is a sampling of cover designs from several recent decades. (Courtesy of Jeanne Youngson)*

Tired and infuriated by unauthorized and unsolicited encroachments, Florence granted her first license for a stage adaptation of *Dracula* to a touring actor-manager named Hamilton Deane, whose family had known Stoker's in Dublin. Deane had quite a following in the provinces, and almost no reputation in London; his barnstorming style was at odds with current taste in the West End. Deane's *Dracula* was conceived as a touring vehicle for less sophisticated regional audiences. Deane originally wanted to play Dracula himself, but eventually realized that Van Helsing was the plummier role with the longest speeches and far more stage time. His wife, Dora Mary Patrick, took the role of Dracula's victim, Mina. The play had its first performance in 1924, and was almost immediately successful. Despite the box office, Deane's and Florence Stoker's relationship was not entirely amicable. "She was very strict," recalled Deane company member Ivan Butler, who never met the lady, but remembered Deane's estimation of her. The widow allowed Deane only a small percentage of the earnings; he compensated with furious touring.

Dracula was a hit in the provinces, but Deane steered clear of the West End for fear of what damage the condescending London critics might wreak on his golden goose. But a fashion for

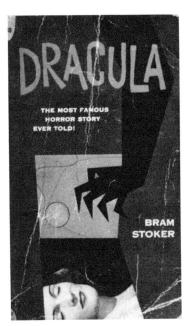

sensational horror plays had recently proved lucrative in the theatre capital, and José Levy, who had successfully produced Sibyl Thorndike's season of Grand Guignol at his Little Theatre in Adelphi, convinced Deane to take a chance. The play opened at the Little in February, 1927, after three seasons of touring.

As Deane feared, the critics did their best to drive a stake through *Dracula*, but it nonetheless "made a hit" among the London populace with its hammy thrills. The flamboyant American publisher and producer Horace Liveright, ever on the prowl for properties with sensational possibilities, liked the premise of *Dracula* but hated the script. He enlisted the American journalist and dramatist John L. Balderston, who had recently scored a success as co-author (with J.C. Squire) of the supernatural romance *Berkeley Square*, to completely rewrite the dialogue for Broadway.

Horace Liveright, the legendary publisher, producer and libertine who brought Dracula to the American stage.

Thereafter, and until World War II, *Dracula* existed in two distinctly different versions, one for British audiences and one for Americans (in point of fact there were three—Florence Stoker commissioned yet another adaptation from a playwright named Charles Morrell which she owned outright—she resented paying adaptor's royalties. But the Morrell play was turgid and talky, and was performed only briefly.) Hamilton Deane's version— published here for the first time—is enjoyably quaint, when not downright campy, and is notable for introducing most of the standard trappings we now associate with *Dracula*: swirling opera capes, French doors, fog machines, secret panels, and, perhaps most memorably, easily-hypnotized maids who can be relied upon to remove a variety of annoyances ranging from crucifixes to garlic flowers to noxious necklaces of vampire-repelling wolfsbane.

Horace Liveright wanted the British actor Raymond Huntley to reprise his West End role of Dracula on Broadway, but the actor refused because of the skimpy salary offered—$150 a week. Rebuffed, Liveright offered even less money to a hungry expatriate actor from Lugos, Hungary, who was in no position to turn down work. And so Béla Ferenc Dezsö Blasko—known professionally as Bela Lugosi—became the strangest matinee idol the New York theatre had ever seen, and was soon to become one of the most instantly identifiable presences in theatrical history.

Dracula enjoyed a two-week tryout in New Haven, Hartford, and other nearby venues in late September 1927 before opening on Broadway October 5. The sheer audacity of the production guaranteed a large box office. Here was a new kind of "mystery play," which, contrary to prevailing stage conventions, did not attempt to "explain away" its terrors as the result of nefarious human agency. *Dracula*, the press releases warned, "deals frankly with the supernatural." Liveright's theatrical manager Louis Cline, a whiz at publicity stunts, had a field day with outrageous and attention-getting promotions. As in London, lobby nurses and fainting patrons were both provided by the management—a conflict of interest, perhaps, but one which drew no serious complaint.

Dracula ran for thirty-three weeks in New York, followed by two simultaneous American tours, one with Bela Lugosi and the other with Raymond Huntley. Liveright mixed and matched his supporting casts so frequently that Louis Cline often refrained from announcing cast members in certain cities, heightening the atmosphere of mystery in the press. (It also allowed him to recycle production photos without regard to the actual performers pictured.) Meanwhile, in England, Hamilton Deane found it necessary to send out three separate touring companies featuring *Dracula*; he called the troupes his "Red," "White," and "Blue" ensembles. Deane tried pairing the vampire melodrama on repertory bills with tried and true chestnuts like *Daddy Longlegs*, and even an adaptation of Mary Shelley's *Frankenstein* by Peggy Webling, but the audience demand for *Dracula* often pushed out everything else. Deane even tried shortening the play in order to squeeze in two evening performances, but the ploy succeeded mostly in exhausting the performers.

The success of the stage play (which earned over $2 million in America alone) brought *Dracula* to the attention of Hollywood, which had shied away from the novel because its sensational horrors had always been considered "unfilmable." A film based on

John L. Balderston, the dramatist and former war correspondent who rewrote Dracula *for Broadway.*

The original three-sheet poster for the Tod Browning production of Dracula *(1931).*

the much tamer thrills of the stage play would be another matter entirely. Following two years of tempestuous negotiations between Florence Stoker, Hamilton Deane, John L. Balderston, their agents, and the studios of Universal, Metro-Goldwyn-Mayer, Columbia and Fox Films, Universal purchased the film rights to the novel and all three existing stage versions of *Dracula* for $40,000 in the summer of 1930. The studio had planned a "superproduction" starring the silent film's "Man of a Thousand Faces," Lon Chaney, in one of his first talking roles. Chaney, however, was terminally ill with cancer, and Universal's plans were thrown into a tailspin. The mounting reality of the Depression forced the financially-strapped Universal to develop a script based almost exclusively on the stage play, and turn to the stage actor Bela Lugosi for a part they originally hoped to give to an established film star. (Lugosi was paid $3,500 for seven weeks of work on the film, and never saw another dime related directly to Universal's *Dracula*, despite his lifelong identification with the part.)

Actor Dwight Frye made the part of Renfield his own with the 1931 film version.

Dracula, directed by Tod Browning, was one of Universal's big moneymakers for 1931, and did its share to save the studio from the economic wolf. The film's success sparked a renewed interest in the stage play. Released to stock in 1930, Deane and Balderston's *Dracula* has been in almost continuous performance somewhere in the world ever since. The play was adapted for vaudeville by Lugosi, who toured it on both coasts in the 1930s. He revived it regularly throughout his career, despite his bitterness that the public didn't care to see him in anything else. For Lugosi, *Dracula* was as much of a curse as a blessing, and when he died in 1956, he was actually buried in the Dracula cloak, medallion and makeup.

The play became a fixture of the regional, college and community theatre circuit. Other stage adaptations of the Stoker novel have since been widely produced (the book itself entered the public domain in the 1950s), but they haven't diminished the power and appeal of the Deane-Balderston collaboration. The play's true renaissance began in 1973, when the Nantucket Stage

A barnstorming Bela frequently made the rounds of stock theatres in the 1940s. (Courtesy of Richard Bojarski)

Company produced a highly stylized version with black-and-white sets and costumes by the illustrator Edward Gorey, whose cobwebby pen-and-ink drawings already had a cult following. It took four years for a Broadway production to be financed (a previously announced co-production with Joseph Papp's New York Shakespeare Festival fell through), but *Dracula* returned triumphantly to Broadway in October 1977 with Frank Langella in the title role. As in 1927, the reviews were not all good—the *New York Times* issued a particularly guarded notice, finding the production lacking in real blood and thunder—but the production defied all critical dismissals and was a major hit in New York and on tour, propelling Langella, like Lugosi, into a film version for Universal, and introducing a whole succession of new Broadway Draculas, including Raul Julia, Jeremy Brett, Jean LeClerc and David Dukes. Terence Stamp took the role in London.

In October 1989, while in London researching my book *Hollywood Gothic: The Tangled Web of "Dracula" from Novel to Stage to Screen*, I had the enormous privilege of interviewing Raymond Huntley, the actor who originated the role for London audiences in 1927 and later toured the states; according to his clippings, he had played the part over 2000 times by 1929, beating out even Bela Lugosi's estimable score (Huntley had had a head start, it should be noted, touring extensively with Hamilton Deane). As he poured tea in his tidy apartment in Pimlico, the sense of being in a time-warp was overwhelming. Bela Lugosi had died an old man when I was only four years old; now, nearing forty, I was sitting in the presence of the man who had turned down the role of Dracula on Broadway, and who was thereby responsible for making Lugosi a star. Huntley had been less than half Lugosi's age — twenty-two to the Hungarian actor's forty-six — which made it possible for us to be sitting in the same room together. Still, it did not seem entirely real.

Huntley told me he was bitter about *Dracula* for several years after he finally doffed the cape; he felt it had limited his possibilities at a crucial period in his career. At eighty-six, John Gielgud and he were the same age, Huntley reminded me, with the implication that, save for the curse of *Dracula*, he, too, might have been a contender in the West End instead of touring the provinces and America as a pantomime devil in a trick coffin. Nonetheless, Huntley had a long and rich career in theatre and films, and was still working the year we spoke.

Bela Lugosi snarls over his $100 per week salary for The Broadway production of Dracula.

The day I finished the manuscript of *Hollywood Gothic*, I felt a sudden compulsion to write the actor and let him know the book was done, and hoping to give him a copy personally when I revisited London. The urgency with which I wrote the letter was a bit strange; I stopped all other work in the middle of a busy day, stamped the letter and took it in person to the post office. For several days after I felt a distinct uneasiness, bordering on dread. And a few days later I picked up the *New York Times* and read Raymond Huntley's obituary. He had died at precisely the time I had written and posted the strangely urgent letter.

Since *Hollywood Gothic*, I have learned quite a bit more about Raymond Huntley, Hamilton Deane, Horace Liveright and Bela Lugosi, much of which is to be found in the book you now hold before you. It is hardly the final curtain on the Dracula story, however — as I write this introduction, filmmakers Francis Ford

Draculabilia: the Deane/ Balderston conception of Dracula has inspired countless derivations and imitations throughout the worlds of merchandising, advertising and communications. (Courtesy of Jeanne Youngson)

Coppola and Roger Corman are readying new adaptations of the legend, and Dracula-related books and memorabilia have become an explosive growth industry. And the *Dracula* centenary in 1997 promises a whole new cycle of revivals, revisitations and reappraisals. One thing is fairly certain: no matter how many 50 million dollar movies are spun out of Bram Stoker's immortal tale, the Deane and Balderston adaptation will continue to be produced on a more modest scale wherever theatre professionals or enthusiastic amateurs have access to an Inverness cape and a dry-ice machine, and wherever audiences are willing to believe, at least for the space of a few hours, Professor Van Helsing's curtain warning that "there are such things!"

And that, in the final analysis, may be the real secret of *Dracula*'s eternal life.

—DAVID J. SKAL
October, 1992

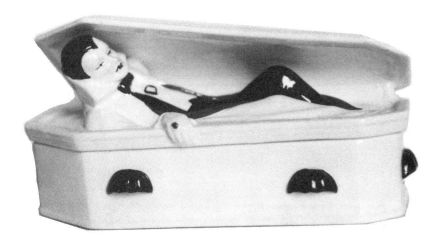

"I saw two red eyes . . . a livid white face . . ." Raymond Huntley and Dora Mary Patrick in the first authorized stage adaptation of Dracula.

Hamilton Deane

Dracula

(1924)

EDITOR'S NOTE

The following version of Hamilton Deane's *Dracula* is based on the
original 1924 script as submitted to the Lord Chamberlain's office,
and a revised text used by Deane's company and circulated by his
agent in 1930. As Deane never intended his script for publication,
his punctuation tended to be idiosyncratic, with run-on phrases of
dialogue broken up by long dashes, etc. For ease of reading, the
editor has added sentence breaks and standard punctuation where
indicated, while retaining the distinctive flavor of
Deane's breathless, headlong style.

Note: Whatever overture is played—the rise of the curtain is to be preceded by three minutes of specially orchestrated Hungarian music, in which the sound of sleigh bells is recurrent.

Prologue

As the curtain rises it discloses the courtyard of a vast ruined castle, from whose tall black windows comes no ray of light, and whose broken battlements show a jagged line against a moon-light sky. Fifteen seconds elapse without sound or movement, and then from the topmost window, centre stage, leans out the figure of a tall thin man, with snow white hair and a long white moustache. His hands and face show "dead white" in the moonlight. Leaning far out of the window, he slowly emerges and crawls down the castle wall face downwards, with his cloak spreading out around him like great wings. As his whole body emerges from the window THE CURTAIN DROPS.

Note for actor playing Dracula:

Trousers must be strapped under feet—one foot to be secured inside window to solid rostrum. The Inverness cape which he wears must be heavily wired, so that when face downwards it assumes the shape of a bat's wings.

Hamilton Deane never actually staged this atmospheric prologue, which proved too expensive and cumbersome for touring. Although the image of Dracula scaling the wall of his castle is one of the most unforgettable images in Stoker's book, it did not appear in a dramatic adaptation until the 1970s.

Opposite: An early dust jacket illustration. (Courtesy of Robert James Leake)

LITTLE THEATRE

JOHN STREET, ADELPHI, STRAND

Lessee and Licensee - - - - - - - - - JOSÉ G. LEVY.

Every Evening at 8.45.
MATINEES: WEDNESDAY & SATURDAY at 2.30

By arrangement with JOSÉ G. LEVY and HENRY MILLAR

HAMILTON DEANE and H. L. WARBURTON

PRESENT

THE VAMPIRE PLAY

"DRACULA"

By HAMILTON DEANE
Adapted from BRAM STOKER'S Famous Novel

Count Dracula ...	...	...	... RAYMOND HUNTLEY
Abraham van Helsing	...	...	... HAMILTON DEANE
Doctor Seward ..	...	...	... STUART LOMATH
Jonathan Harker	...	...	... BERNARD GUEST
Quincy P. Morris	...	...	... FRIEDA HEARN
Lord Godalming	...	...	... PETER JACKSON
R. M. Renfield ...	...	...	... BERNARD JUKES (By Courtesy of Percy Hutchison Esq.)
The Warder ...	...	...	... JACK HOWARTH
The Parlourmaid	...	...	... KILDA MACLEOD
The Housemaid	...	...	... BETTY MURGATROYD
Mina Harker ...	...	...	··· DORA MARY PATRICK

Act One

The study of JONATHAN HARKER's *house on Hampstead Heath. An ordinary enough looking room but furnished with taste, and bearing evidence of a woman's hand in the arrangement of the furniture. There are folding doors centre. The entrance to the dining room is upper left. The fireplace is right and has a broad club fender, and two large armchairs are close by. A full-sized mirror is over mantelpiece. There is another door above fireplace upper right. A roomy Chesterfield is set square to and actually touching wall left.*

The time is just before dinner. The season is mid-winter. The period is today.

As the curtain rises, DOCTOR SEWARD *enters right. He comes briskly down stage and consults his watch, he then crosses to fireplace and compares watch with the clock on mantelpiece. He stands for a few seconds drumming impatiently with his fingers on mantelpiece.* JONATHAN HARKER *enters.*

SEWARD: Well, how is she now?

HARKER: No change. Pale and listless, but doing her best to keep up a show of brightness.

SEWARD: Well this thing has beaten me. First of all Lucy and now your wife. In all my experience as a medical man I've never seen anything like it. I've tried everything I know of to get at the cause of it all, and now I'm back to where I started.

HARKER: My God, if only your friend the scientist would come!

SEWARD: I wrote him days ago describing the case fully—had a wire this morning—and I'm expecting him any minute now.

HARKER: You have great confidence in him, Seward? [*Sits on couch.*]

SEWARD: He's an old friend, and master of mine, Professor Van Helsing of Amsterdam, who knows as much about obscure diseases as anyone in the world. He would, I know, do anything for me, for a personal reason, and we must just accept his wishes.

Seemingly he is an arbitrary man. But this is only because he knows what he is talking about. He's a philosopher and a meta-physician, one of the most advanced scientists of his day, and he has an absolutely open mind.

HARKER: Well, it seems to me that when a man of your experience admits he's up against it—this Van Helsing will have need of all his science to diagnose the case. By the way, Mina wanted to come down to dinner, but I persuaded her to let me send some up to her. She's dreadfully weak—and as Van Helsing is certain to want to see her tonight, she'll have to husband her strength.

SEWARD: Quite right, I'll have to see Van Helsing first—and give him all the details, then afterwards no doubt he'll want to see her—he's not the man to waste a moment.

HARKER: [*Ringing bell.*] The gong will be going for dinner in a moment. [*Enter* MAID.] Professor Van Helsing's room is ready, isn't it?

MAID: Yes, sir.

HARKER: Well, directly he comes show him in here.

MAID: And shall I call you, sir?

HARKER: No. Doctor Seward will see him first.

MAID: Very good, sir. [*Exit.*]

SEWARD: Where are the others?

HARKER: Quincy Morris is upstairs, dressing, and you know Count Dracula never eats a thing after sunset. I left him just now superintending the placing of his extraordinary baggage in the coach house at Carfax.

SEWARD: What baggage?

HARKER: Well, he arrived here with very little personal belongings—his whole interest seems to be centred in the transference from his castle in Transylvania of several huge packing cases, two he brought with him—the rest arrived since.

SEWARD: He's bought this place next door, then?

HARKER: Yes—I put the deal through for him two days ago. There are only one or two formalities to be gone through now.

SEWARD: Strange, isn't it, that he and I should occupy the houses on either side of yours—my Lunatic Asylum is bare and gloomy enough in all conscience—but I wouldn't take a pension and live in Carfax. It's the gloomiest place I've ever seen; they tell me the house dates back to medieval times—is falling in in places and is inches thick in dust.

HARKER: Well, there is no accounting for tastes. I did my best to put

Hamilton Deane and Dora Mary Patrick in one of their many co-starring vehicles. (Courtesy of Ivan Butler)

him off taking the place. But he was determined; so, as his man of business, I just had to go ahead with the purchase.

[*Gong sounds.*]

Ready, old man? We'll be a dull party at dinner tonight—just a few puzzled and anxious men.

SEWARD: You must buck up Harker—don't forget—there's Van Helsing.

[SEWARD *and* HARKER *pass into dining room. The* MAID *enters—picks up cushions on Chesterfield, shakes them out and replaces them. Picks up a book from armchair and places it on table—looks round room, switches out lights. Simultaneously the green spot line goes on, and the figure of* DRACULA *is facing her—gives a slight scream and switches on the lights again— he does not move but speaks in a reassuring way.*]

DRACULA: I have sorrow if I have given to you the alarm—perhaps

Newspaper cartoon of the London cast of Dracula. *(Courtesy of Richard Bojarski)*

my foot-fall sounds not so heavy as that of your English ploughman.

MAID: It's all right, sir. I just did not see you come in.

DRACULA: Look at me — is it not so that you have recently suffered from a form of Malaise — the Neuralgia — you call it so?

MAID: Well, yes, sir, the last few days I have had a sharp pain in my forehead and temples running down sometimes to the neck.

DRACULA: I can give — I can take away — would it be a matter for you of gratitude that I should instantly remove this pain?

MAID: What do you mean, sir? I don't understand.

DRACULA: Of what grade your intelligence may be, I know not — but it is of truth that the pain would yield to the Hypnotic Suggestion.

MAID: Excuse me, sir, but if you propose to cure me by such methods, I would rather have the pain.

DRACULA: I see you have the customary bucolic idea of Mesmeric Suggestion — a waving of arms and many "passes" — my method is of contrary — simple, direct and instantaneously effective.

[*As he speaks he indicates with a gesture of the hand that the girl should look at him — she does so — his whole manner changes — bending down over her — he stares straight into her eyes placing the left thumb against her forehead — she makes one attempt to remove his hand then remains quiescent — after a pause of three seconds he speaks and his manner to her has completely changed.*]

So! You are more easy of impression — even than I imagined — listen to me — from now on you do my bidding — "Volition" of will — of your own accord you have none. Answer! Are you in accord with me?

MAID: I– – –! [*She mumbles something altogether incoherent.*]

DRACULA: There is on his way to this house a man whose "will" is at cross-purposes to my own — crush him I shall, but I have need of material help — that need *you* will supply — you may go now — but remember that any suggestion emanating from my brain you will instantly adopt.

[MAID *covers her face with her hands and gives a low moan.*]

The time has come! [*He moves slowly towards the window curtains — he turns and says:*] When my brain says "Come" you will cross land or sea to do my bidding. When "I will" you to do a thing it shall be done. [*Exit.*]

"I can give—I can take away ..." Dracula (Raymond Huntley) impresses the parlour-maid with the force of his personality. Caricature by Tom Titt.

AT THE PLAY.

"DRACULA" (LITTLE).

THE late Mr. BRAM STOKER's *Dracula*, which I understand has for many years been a cause of frequent nightmares in the unsophisticated, has been done into a play by Mr. HAMILTON DEANE, and I am bound to say that he has made a mirth-provoking affair of it—in parts. It is true this vampire business is not primarily designed for mirth, and no doubt the apparatus of suddenly-opened doors, clocks that tick eerily, howling lunatics who eat flies and white mice, pink-eyed bats (not induced by alcohol), magnesium flashes, swirling mists which don't smell at all like mists, pale-faced aristocratic aliens whose bodies are not reflected in plane mirrors and whose hair is twisted into devilish horns may very well be more seriously alarming between the pages of a book than they are in the three-dimensional medium of the stage. If this had all been played in a full-blooded transpontine manner, and if everything had not been said seven times, laughter would have been even more easy, though I admit there was something especially diverting in watching a company of grave conscientious actors in the West-End manner heroically pretending to take it all seriously.

Of course *Jonathan Harker* was asking for trouble when he shared a semi-detached house with *Doctor Seward*, who apparently kept or didn't keep his loosely-controlled lunatics in the other half of it. And it was tempting Providence to let the house on his other side to so obviously sinister a person as *Count Dracula*, with his mysterious packing-cases, his horned hair, red eyes and gaping fangs. But he couldn't be expected, I suppose, to realise that his sister-in-law would fade away to the grave, after I know not how many unavailing transfusions of blood, with those queer tiny wounds in her throat. And it was certainly rough luck that his own wife should apparently be going the same dreadful way. Not at all surprising that *Doctor Seward* (who looked and talked less like a medical man than seemed humanly possible) should be puzzled. Mere mumps would have puzzled him, I feel sure.

But help is at hand. *Professor Abraham van Helsing*, the Dutchman—psychologist, psycho-analyst, hypnotist and were-wolf specialist—arrives. His diagnosis is that a vampire is at work. Nonsense? Not at all. We scientific men know a good many queer things, let us tell you. He interviews the deplorable *Count*, having learnt about the packing-cases, which from his specialised knowledge he recognises

as the lairs or changing-places necessary to every self-respecting practising vampire; offers him garlic, a herb notoriously fatal to vampires (and other non-Fascists), and sees the violent convulsions into which it throws him; after which he brilliantly concludes that the red-eyed nobleman may have something to do with the sad business. "Of course I can't be sure, mind you, but——"; the cautious scientific attitude in fact. This is, as you have guessed, a frightfully scientific play.

The heroine is visibly sinking. Shall we be in time to save her? The astute *Van Helsing*, having further cheered the patient and her friends by explaining what a perfectly terrible condition she is in and how lucky she is to have him there; having removed and sterilised (with garlic) all the *Count's* lairs but the one in the coach-house next-door; having explained to *Lord Godalming* that it is necessary that his late *fiancée*, *Lucy*, must have her tomb broken into and a stake driven into her heart in order to prevent her going about as a "beau'ful lady" (a were-wolf in fact), nibbling the

throats of the Hampstead young—she is "undead" and must be made "true dead"; having carefully decorated poor *Mrs. Harker* with garlic and hung a cross about her neck, which the maid, hypnotised by *Dracula*, removes in a trance, thus leaving the vampire free for his hasty evening meal; having with his three friends surrounded the *Count* aforesaid and tried vainly to impress him with four fore-fingers dramatically levelled at him, he countering with a firework, under cover of which he makes his escape—it only remains for the four heroes to track the beast to his lair in the coach-house and at the precise hour of sunset to shine four green bulls'-eyes upon him and plunge a stake into his heart so that his tortured soul may leave his body with a fizz in a cloud of smoke.

For us it only remains to sidle quietly into the Adelphi, wondering sadly why this sort of thing should be supposed to be adequate entertainment for adults in this year of grace in one of the world's capital cities.   T.

HYPNOTISING "NIPPY."

"You shall come across continents to serve me."

Count Dracula . . Mr. RAYMOND HUNTLEY.
The Parlourmaid . MISS KILDA MACLEOD.

[THE MAID *stands staring straight in front of her, then with an effort she pulls herself together and moves towards the folding doors, looking back over the right shoulder — passes through the folding doors and to left, leaving doors wide open. A few seconds' pause and she re-enters, preceding* PROFESSOR VAN HELSING *who enters briskly looking sharply to right and left as he does so. He is a man of medium height, slightly built, in the early fifties, with a clean-shaven face, chiefly distinguished by shaggy red-grey eyebrows and a mass of red-grey hair, which without a parting falls backwards showing a high forehead. His dark eyes are set widely apart; and the whole man brings with him an air of resolution and quick, decisive action. He wears an overcoat and a heavy muffler, and is removing gloves as he comes in.*]

The original program cover.

VAN HELSING: This is the house of Mr. Jonathan Harker — is that not so?

MAID: Yes, sir. But I was to inform Dr. Seward the moment you arrived.

VAN HELSING: That is well. [*He looks at her keenly.*] What startled you just now, my child?

MAID: Oh, nothing, sir. [*She looks surprised.*] I'll tell Dr. Seward you've come. Won't you sit down, sir?

VAN HELSING: [*Looking hard at her, then round the room.*] If you will be so good.

[*Exit* MAID. VAN HELSING *then turns to greet* DR. SEWARD, *who enters.*]

SEWARD: Well, this is wonderful of you, Van Helsing. We have been on pins and needles for fear you couldn't come.

[*They shake hands.*]

VAN HELSING: Ah! friend John — when that time you sucked from my wound so swiftly the poison of the gangrene, without even a thought as to what might happen to yourself if there were the "ever-so-tiniest" cut on your lips — you make of Van Helsing a friend for life. What I can do — I do for you, my friend.

SEWARD: You don't know what your coming means to me — to all of us. We are in sore straits here. But I say, I am forgetting — you must be starving. Won't you come right in now to dinner?

VAN HELSING: Friend John — I have gathered from your letter there is not much time to lose. While there is work to be done — I think not much of the sleep or of the eating. Besides I have forestalled the matter by dining shortly after mid-day on the boat — so you my friend will sit down and give me the facts in this case — I will enquire the details later.

> [SEWARD *motions* VAN HELSING *to Chesterfield.* VAN HELS-ING *sits — and* SEWARD *sits facing him but on the arm of Chesterfield, he takes cigarette from pocket and offers it to* VAN HELSING.]

VAN HELSING: I no smoke my friend — I listen.

> [SEWARD *lights cigarette and obviously arranges his ideas in sequence.*]

SEWARD: Well! Our host and hostess are a Mr. and Mrs. Jonathan Harker. He is a well-to-do solicitor and man of affairs — my place — the Lunatic Asylum, you know — is just over there [*Indicates 100 yards away.*] I've been a close friend of the family for quite some time — in fact the Harkers, Lord Godalming, Miss Morris, an American, Mrs. Harker's greatest friend Lucy West-

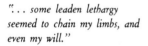

". . . some leaden lethargy seemed to chain my limbs, and even my will."

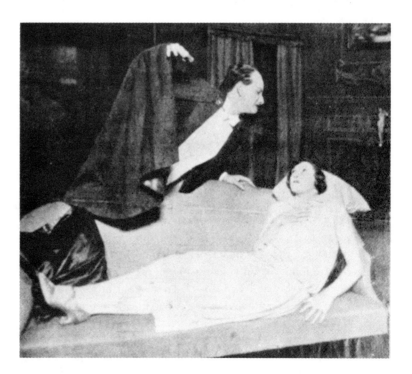

era and myself have for some years past formed a little "coterie" of our own, and have been pretty nearly inseparable. We had great times together—and I'd better tell you now—as you're certain to guess it, that Godalming and myself were deeply in love with Lucy Westera—she was without exception the most perfect woman.

VAN HELSING: Yes—I listen to that later—with your facts I beg of you to go on.

SEWARD: Well—Godalming proved to be the lucky one—and I just sunk naturally into the background, but in no way did it interfere with our friendship.

VAN HELSING: You accepted the inevitable—yes?

SEWARD: Well, six weeks ago the Harkers had a "house-party" consisting of the usual "set", with only one stranger, a Count Dracula from Transylvania who had been staying here whilst Harker, who is his man of business, arranged the purchase of several lots of property in different parts of London for his client.

VAN HELSING: And the Count—you like him, eh?

SEWARD: Well I can't say I do. I feel "on edge" whenever he comes near me. But apart from that and the fact that he is a most peculiar chap, I have nothing against him—he is a courtly, cultured man, with a manner that belongs to another period—I nearly said another world.

VAN HELSING: Well—yes—and what happened?

SEWARD: Two days after the house party had come together—Lucy was taken ill, just a slow fading away—she ate and slept well, but grew weaker and more languid every day, at night she gasped as for air. I could easily see she was bloodless—and yet there were none of the usual anaemic signs and the qualitative analysis gave quite a normal condition.

VAN HELSING: Did you not think of performing blood transfusion?

SEWARD: When things were desperate. Yes. [Baring forearm.] You see this mark? Well, Godalming and Miss Morris have the same.

VAN HELSING: So-o-o, three transfusions. And the effect?

SEWARD: After each she rallied wonderfully, the colour returned to her cheeks—and I would feel morally certain she had turned the corner, but the following morning she would again be ashy pale, and the bloodless symptoms would return, only more marked than before. On the morning of the tenth day it was plain she could not rally—and that evening at sunset she passed away.

VAN HELSING: And of external abrasions there were none, eh?

SEWARD: None whatever, except for two marks on the throat.

Like many of the names in Stoker's novel, Lucy Westenra's underwent several metamorphoses in stage and film adaptations. Westenra (meaning "Light of the West") became both "Westera" and "Westeura" in variant texts of Deane's adaptation. In Balderston's re-write, the surname was dropped, the Mina character being renamed Lucy Seward. Tod Browning's 1931 film reinstated the original Lucy/Mina relationship, but Lucy's last name was changed again, this time to Weston.

Twenty-two-year-old Horace Raymond Huntley (who never used his first name professionally) in a publicity portrait at the time of his stage success in Dracula.

VAN HELSING: [*Rising quickly.*] On the throat, eh? What like were they?

SEWARD: Just two tiny wounds like little white dots—with red centres.

VAN HELSING: And you tell me that the symptoms of Madame Harker are precisely the same?

SEWARD: Precisely. Two mornings after poor Lucy was buried— Harker had the greatest difficulty in arousing his wife—she was so sound asleep that for several seconds she didn't recognise him, but stared at him with a sort of blank terror, as one looks who had been waked out of a bad dream—since then, she, like Lucy, has been sinking rapidly, and is growing worse daily, and yet I can do nothing for her, that's why I sent for you.

VAN HELSING: Thank God you did, and now, my good friend John, let me caution you—you deal with the madmen—you tell not them what you do, or what you think—so deal with the rest of the world. You and I shall keep as yet what we know—here. [*Touching forehead.*] I have for myself thoughts for the present, which later I shall unfold to you, but now—we have not even minutes to waste—it is necessary that I see Madame Harker at once.

SEWARD: [*Ringing bell.*] She is quite ready for you—she—like the rest of us—has been counting the minutes till you came.

[MAID *enters.*]

MAID: Yes, sir?

SEWARD: Would you ask Mrs. Harker to be kind enough to come down to the study now?

MAID: Yes, sir. [*Exits.*]

VAN HELSING: Friend John—I would wish to see Madame Harker alone. Would you be so kind as to pass to me that little bag, [*Indicating bag with which he entered the room.*] which contains the ghastly paraphernalia of our beneficial trade.

[SEWARD *places bag on table by Chesterfield.* VAN HELSING *opens it as* MINA HARKER *enters, leaning on the arm of her* MAID. SEWARD *goes to her other side at once and the three stand facing* VAN HELSING *while* SEWARD *introduces him to Mrs. Harker.* MINA HARKER *is a tall, well developed girl of about twenty-four. She has a broad and high forehead and steadfast eyes. At the moment she is ghastly and chalkily white, the red seems to have gone from her lips; she speaks and moves with obvious difficulty.*]

SEWARD: Mina, may I present to you Professor Helsing who has
come from Holland to take care of you.

MINA: I can't say how grateful we all are to you for coming, Doctor.

[VAN HELSING *and* SEWARD *help* MINA *down to Chesterfield.
She sits. Exit* MAID.]

VAN HELSING: Ah! Madame — I am only too happy to be of use to any
friend of my good friend John. They told me that you have been
down in the spirit and that you were of a ghastly pale. To them I
say "pouf". How can he [*Pointing to* SEWARD.] know anything of
young ladies. He has his madmen to play with — and to bring them
back to happiness. But the young ladies! He has neither wife nor
daughter, and the young do not tell themselves to the young, but
to the old, like me, who have seen so many sorrows and the causes
of them. So my dear we will send him away while you and I have a
little talk all to ourselves.

SEWARD: All right — goodbye for the present Mina — I leave you in
good hands. [*Exits.*]

VAN HELSING: Will Madame permit? [*He takes her pulse and closely
examines her lips and lower eye-lids during the following dialogue.*] And
now — when first did you notice anything unusual in your health?

*Van Helsing (Hamilton Deane)
examines Mina (Dora Mary
Patrick) in an attempt to solve
the mystery of her unnatural
pallor. (Courtesy of Jeanne
Youngson)*

MINA: Two nights after poor Lucy Westera was buried—I had a terrible dream.

VAN HELSING: A dream—yes—tell me of it.

MINA: I can't quite remember how I fell asleep that night. I remember hearing the sudden barking of dogs and a lot of queer sounds. And then there was silence over everything, silence so profound that it startled me, and I got up and looked out of the window— not a thing seemed to be stirring—except a thin streak of white mist, that crept with almost imperceptible slowness towards the house. When I got back to bed I felt a lethargy creeping over me. I lay a while—but could not sleep, so I got up and looked out of the window again. The mist was spreading and was now close to the house, so that I could see it lying thick against the wall, as though it were stealing up to the windows. Then I must have fallen asleep, for except dreams, I don't remember anything till the morning—

As a condition of his employment, Raymond Huntley was required to provide his own evening clothes for *Dracula* on an initial salary of eight pounds a week. "God knows how much it cost," he recalled in 1989. "I couldn't really tell you how I managed it, but somehow I did."

"At last ... the pleasure of seeing you alone." Raymond Huntley displays his unholy wares to a horrified Dora Mary Patrick. (Courtesy of the Dracula Society)

when my husband woke me. My dreams were very peculiar—I thought that I was asleep and waiting for my husband to come back. Then it began to dawn on me that the air was heavy and dank, and cold. I put back the clothes from my face and found to my surprise that all was dim around me. The electric light which I had left on for my husband came only like a tiny red spark through the fog, which had evidently grown thicker and poured into the room—some leaden lethargy seemed to chain my limbs, and even my will. The mist grew thicker and thicker. I could see it, like smoke, pouring in through the window and then through the fog I saw two red eyes staring at me and a livid white face bending over me—out of the mist. Oh, God! it was horrible—horrible!

VAN HELSING: Come, Madame—I beg you to be calm. We shall see that these so unpleasant dreams trouble you not again.

MINA: The next morning I felt weak and languid—some part of my life seemed to have ebbed from me—that night nothing happened, but the following night and every night since then—has come the mist—the red eyes—and that awful face, until now, I dread the night time—the dreams—and the weakness that comes to me always in my sleep. I know that all this sounds ridiculous in the telling, but please, professor, do not laugh at what I have told you—I couldn't bear it.

VAN HELSING: Nay—I am not likely to laugh. This is no jest—but life and death, perhaps more!

MINA: What do you mean, Professor?

VAN HELSING: I think, my dear young lady, that the smuts in London are not quite so bad as they used to be—when I was a student here. Will Madame allow me?

> [*Places a cushion under* MINA's *head—then gently lays her head back on it—as he does so he deliberately but gently pulls down the velvet band around her throat—and discloses the two white marks—with red centres—which she has tried to conceal.*]

Do not move, Madame!

> [*He takes a small magnifying glass from bag at side and examines the wounds carefully.*]

So-o-o. [*He draws his breath in with a hiss.*] Madame, you will tell me—how long these so small marks on your throat have been there.

"Mr. Deane cannot write dialogue," complained *The Morning Post.* "He does not begin to understand what dramatic dialogue is, and sometimes he gets an unintended comic effect by sheer pomposity of speech. . . . Much of the acting, too, by a company not one member of which was known to a London audience, was of the gifted amateur type. Several of the cast were clearly suffering from prolonged bouts of elocution: they enunciated clearly in a monotonous manner each and every syllable, giving all syllables the same weight and value. A lady talked about her Leth Are Gee." Nonetheless, the *Post* admitted, "in spite of prolixity, of toneless acting, of undramatic dialogue, the play extraordinarily gripped and scared the audience. Those who like to be horribly thrilled will be horribly thrilled by *Dracula.*"

W.E. Holloway made a popular touring Dracula for Hamilton Deane in the late twenties.

MINA: Since — that morning!

VAN HELSING: I thank you, Madame — and now — if you will excuse me — I will make what preparations I may to guard against a recurrence of these — ah — dreams! But first you will tell me of your bedroom — which floor it is on — how many windows are there — and which part of the grounds do they overlook?

MINA: It's on the first floor, directly over this room — from the corridor you enter my boudoir — and the bedroom itself leads off the boudoir and has but one window — there is also but one window in the boudoir itself.

VAN HELSING: And from which of these did you see the mist rising?

MINA: From the boudoir window.

VAN HELSING: Thank you, Madame — I would wish to meet your husband, and the other occupants of this house — but you will be so good as to remain on the ground floor — and not enter the boudoir until such time as I have been there — and have seen to one or two little things. Is it permitted that I ring the bell Madame? [*Rings bell.*]

MINA: Of course — I fancy that my husband and the other men are impatiently waiting to see you. [*Enter* MAID.] Would you please tell Mr. Harker that Doctor Van Helsing is ready to see him now.

MAID: Yes, Madame. [*Exit.*]

VAN HELSING: Now, my dear lady, I beg of you to rest all you can — you will have need of all your strength and courage.

[*Enter* SEWARD, *followed by* JONATHAN HARKER, LORD GODALMING *and* MISS MORRIS.]

Ah friend John — and which is the husband of this so brave lady?

SEWARD: [*Introducing.*] This is Jonathan Harker — Professor Van Helsing.

HARKER: [*Steps forward and grips* VAN HELSING'*s hand in both of his.*] Thank God you've come, sir.

SEWARD: And this is Miss Morris from the Lone Star State of U.S.A.

VAN HELSING: My dear Miss Morris, you should be proud of your great State — some day we shall hear much of Texas, when the Pole and the Tropics may hold allegiance to the Stars and Stripes.

SEWARD: And this is Lord Godalming — Dr. Van Helsing.

VAN HELSING: Ah — my Lord Godalming — I had the "so-great-honour" to know your father when he was a member of the Wyndham. I grieve to know by your holding the title that he is no more.

[*Suddenly* MINA *gets up from couch staring straight in front of her and speaks in a dull, mechanical voice.*]

MINA: I must go — he is calling me — he is calling me!

[*With arms outstretched she turns to the right and moves towards centre door — looking neither to the right nor to the left — the men who are grouped around her fall back in amazement — except* VAN HELSING *who, after one long look at her face, gently takes her arm and says persuasively:*]

VAN HELSING: Not now Madame — you will do what I say. [*Sharply to* HARKER.] You will ring that bell.

[SEWARD *rings the bell.*]

MINA: Let me go! Please let me go! He is calling me!

VAN HELSING: Not yet, madame — you are much too tired — is it not so? You will rest quietly in the next room — with your maid, till I

In Stoker's novel, Quincey Morris was one of Lucy Westenra's suitors, a strapping Texan who loses his life along with Dracula at the story's climax. The role was transformed and trans-sexualized by Deane to provide another female part for his company. In contemporary productions of *Dracula*, the part of Dr. Seward is often played as a woman for reasons of practical casting.

Twenty-four-year-old Ivan Butler as he appeared in the role of Lord Godalming for the Hamilton Deane Company. Below, Butler in the title role following World War II. (Courtesy of Ivan Butler)

come for you. [MAID *enters*.] You will please take Madame to the next room—see that she is comfortable and you will not leave her on any pretext whatever—above all, answer no bells—you understand?

MAID: Quite, sir. Will you come with me, Madame.

> [MAID *leads* MINA *gently off.* MINA *does not turn towards audience again—but goes limply out. As the door closes* VAN HELSING *turns to the other men, his face is very grave—and he drops entirely his urbane bed-side manner.*]

VAN HELSING: Young Madame is very bad. Very bad. If what I suspect as to the cause of her illness is true—then we have not a moment to lose, Mr. Harker. Is there in your house a domestic you can trust? I would have him go to a certain district in Soho, and obtain for me on prescription something I need at once—from my friend Vanderpool of Haarlem.

MORRIS: Say, Professor—I should be tickled to death to do anything to help. Just hand over that prescription—and I'll be back in no time!

VAN HELSING: It is good. [*Writing.*] This is the address—and here is the prescription—you will receive it in the form of a parcel, and I beg of you, my friend, to lose no time.

MORRIS: You can count on me. [*Exit.*]

VAN HELSING: Ha! She is good—that American.

GODALMING: Look here, Professor, I don't know what you suspect, or what you know about this case—but if there is anything on earth that I can do—please give me a chance to do it.

VAN HELSING: I am afraid that I shall have need of the help, and above all the confidence of all of you. There are black times ahead of us, and you, Mr. Harker, will have need of all your courage and belief. At the moment I would wish to speak alone to my friend John here—so perhaps you, Mr. Harker, and Lord Godalming would be so good as to remain with Madame, and if there is sign— the slightest—that she behave as just now—you will call me at once.

HARKER: Professor—tell me one thing before we go—is there any immediate danger?

VAN HELSING: There is immediate danger, my friend. And it is for me to discover from what source the danger comes—and ward him off. I have the great belief in the power of Good over Evil—the devil may work against us—all he can—but God sends us help when we have need of it.

HARKER: God grant [*Taking* VAN HELSING'*s hand.*] that the help we need so badly, came in your form tonight.

GODALMING: Come along, old man. [*To* VAN H.] We'll let you know if there is the slightest change in Mrs. Harker.

> [HARKER *and* GODALMING *exit. Immediately they have gone,* VAN HELSING *turns quickly to* SEWARD.]

VAN HELSING: Do you mean to tell me friend John, that you have no suspicion as to what poor Miss Lucy died of?

SEWARD: Of nervous prostration, following on great loss, or waste of blood.

VAN HELSING: You are clever man, friend John—you reason well, but you are too prejudiced—you do not let your eyes see nor your ears hear—and that which is outside your daily life is not of account to you. There are things which you cannot understand, and yet which are! Some people see things that others cannot. I suppose now— you do not believe in corporeal transference. No? Nor Astral bodies. No? Can you tell me why—when other spiders die small and soon—that one great spider lived for centuries in the tower of the old Spanish church—and grew and grew, till, on descending he could drink the oil of all the church lamps? Can you tell me why—in the Pampas, aye, and elsewhere, there are bats that come at night and open the veins of cattle and horses and suck dry their veins? How in some islands of the Western Seas, there are bats which hang on the trees all day, and that when the sailors sleep on the deck, because it is hot, flit down on them, and then—and then, in the morning are found dead men—white as even Miss Lucy was?

Vampire bat emblem from a 1927 edition of Dracula's Guest.

SEWARD: Good God, Professor, do you mean to tell me that Lucy was bitten by such a bat, and such a thing is here in London in the Twentieth Century?

VAN HELSING: [*Waves him to silence.*] Can you tell me why men in all ages and places, believe that there are some few who live on always if they be permit. That there are men and women who cannot die. Can you tell me how the Indian fakir can make himself to die, and have been buried, and his grave sealed, and corn sowed on it, and then men come and take away the unbroken seal, and that there lie the Indian fakir not dead—but that rise up and walk amongst them as before. My friend, I do so want you to believe!

SEWARD: Believe in what?

VAN HELSING: To believe in things you cannot! I heard once of an American who so defined "Faith" as "That which enables us to believe things which we *know* to be *untrue*."

SEWARD: In God's name, Van Helsing, what do you mean?

VAN HELSING: I mean this friend John—that the death of Miss Lucy and the present illness of Madame Mina, is the work of a "Were-Wolf" or Vampire. How he comes, or in what form—I know not—it is for me to find out—but this I know, and that is how to ward him off. And that is why at the present moment our good friend Miss Morris is procuring for me in Soho—a parcel of garlic with which I decorate the room of Madame. The "Nosferatu" or "Un-dead" like not Garlic any more than they like the symbol of the Christian faith—the Crucifix!

SEWARD: Van Helsing—this is awful—what on earth are we to do?

VAN HELSING: Take steps to guard Madame now—and after—there remains a greater task, to find the author of all this, and to stamp him out—it is a long task and a difficult, and there is danger in it and pain. Shall you not help me, friend John! But in order to do so—*you must believe!*

SEWARD: As you said, Van Helsing—these things are altogether outside my daily life—but whatever else I believe in—I have the greatest faith in YOU—you've only got to command me, and remember I'm with you to the end.

> [*As* SEWARD *finishes speaking—a long low wail comes from the outside of the window—it is a human voice—but tails off into the semblance of the howl of a wolf.*]

VAN HELSING: What is that?

SEWARD: Oh, it is nothing to be alarmed about—it comes from my lunatic asylum over there—it is a patient of mine named Renfield, whose case interests me exceedingly. He's so quaint, in his ideas, and so unlike the usual lunatic that I just can't understand him. He's morbidly excitable, has periods of gloom, ending in some fixed idea which I can't make out. For two years he's been the best behaved patient I've got—but since the night we first noticed Lucy's illness, his behaviour has become quite unaccountable. He breaks out of his room on every conceivable occasion. But I don't worry about that, as he never goes far—his main idea seems to be to get into this place—Carfax—on the other side of the house here.

VAN HELSING: That's the newly acquired property of Harker's guest,

Florence Stoker's outrage over the plagiarized German film adaptation Nosferatu (1922), *prompted her to formally license the dramatic rights to Hamilton Deane. Though she secured a court order for the destruction of the film's negative, Mrs. Stoker was unable to completely suppress the film. Above, an impression of actor Max Schreck in the title role by the film's production designer, Albin Grau.*

Count Dracula, is it not?

SEWARD: Yes.

VAN HELSING: And so your patient's increased dementia was co-incident with the arrival of the Count.

SEWARD: It would seem to be, but of course it may be mere coincidence.

VAN HELSING: Tell me, what are the main features of his mania?

SEWARD: Well, he seems to have some settled scheme of his own. I imagine he is abnormally cruel. He uses half his food as a means of catching flies, then having acquired an enormous quantity of them, he turns his attention to spiders, and feeds them with flies. The other day, I found he had managed to get hold of some sparrows — and already the spiders have diminished.

VAN HELSING: He is evidently a "Zoophagous" — a "life-eating" maniac — he desires to absorb as many lives as he can, and does it in a cumulative way. He gave many flies to one spider, and many spiders to one bird — I wonder what his next step will be.

SEWARD: I can tell you that — this morning he begged me to let him have a kitten — but why are you so particularly interested in this man's case when you have so much more of importance to think about?

The insect-eating Renfield, as caricatured by E.S. Hynes.

VAN HELSING: The ever so tiniest detail of anyone in, or near, this house is of vital interest to me at the moment.

SEWARD: Well, if you'll excuse me I must go and see to this patient of mine — I expect the attendants have him under lock and key by now.

VAN HELSING: You are going — very well — I smoke a pipe and do some thinking, but perhaps you will permit me to see and speak with your patient some time — I am interested in him.

SEWARD: Why certainly — of course — any time you are ready to see him. [*Exit.*]

> [VAN HELSING *goes slowly to table by Chesterfield and from his bag he produces a Dutch pipe and a square of tobacco case and he crosses to fireplace catching sight of his reflection in mirror over mantelpiece. He pauses, and with his pipe in his right hand, he apostrophises his reflection.*]

VAN HELSING: Ah, my friend, you have your work cut out this time.

> [*As* VAN HELSING *speaks the side door left opens and* COUNT DRACULA *walks quietly down to fireplace. He stops beside* VAN HELSING *but slightly upstage so that he is opposite the upper half of mirror which is* blind *and throws no reflection.*]

DRACULA: Is that so?

VAN HELSING: [*Turning suddenly — dropping pipe and tobacco.*] The Devil!

DRACULA: Oh, come — not as bad as that.

VAN HELSING: Your pardon — but you startled me — I presume you are Count Dracula?

DRACULA: I am Dracula!

VAN HELSING: [*Holding out his hand.*] My name is Van Helsing.

> [*As* DRACULA *shakes hands with him* VAN HELSING *withdraws his hand quickly and represses a shudder as though the physical contact was distasteful to him.* DRACULA *notices this and smiles slightly —* VAN HELSING *looks him in the face and turns to mirror — and registers the fact that no reflection of* DRACULA *exists. He turns his back to fireplace and addresses* DRACULA.]

VAN HELSING: It is strange that you should have so startled me just now — for I was looking in the mirror — and the reflection covers the whole room.

DRACULA: Ah the mirror — it is a foul bauble of man's vanity.

The original hand-lettered cover of Hamilton Deane's prompt-book. (Courtesy of the Dracula Society)

Dracula (Raymond Huntley) suspects that Van Helsing (Sam Livesey) may have a trick up his sleeve. (Courtesy of the Dracula Society)

[DRACULA *picks up one of the heavy candlesticks from mantelpiece and makes a movement as though to smash the mirror—then suddenly changing his mind, he examines the candlestick critically, and replaces it gently.*] And so you are the scientist of much learning, who has come from the land of the tulip—to care for our charming hostess?

VAN HELSING: That is undoubtedly my business, Count.

DRACULA: I wish you success in your endeavours. [VAN HELSING *bows slightly.*] As for me I am a stranger in a strange land. But I have grown to love this great London with its teeming millions—so different from my own land of Transylvania, where the sparseness of the population gives one little scope.

VAN HELSING: Scope for what, Count?

DRACULA: For my purpose! So after centuries of waiting, I have at last found my way to England.

VAN HELSING: Centuries!

DRACULA: A figure of speech, my friend. I have purchased through our worthy host, Mr. Harker, the house and grounds called Carfax. I am glad that it is old and big—I am glad that there is a chapel of old times. We Transylvania nobles love not to think that our bones may lie amongst the common dead. I am no longer young, and my heart is not attuned to mirth. Moreover, the walls of my castle are broken, and the shadows are many, and the wind breathes cold through the broken battlements. I love the shade—and the shadow—and would be alone with my thoughts when I may.

VAN HELSING: But I do not understand. If you seek solitude, why come to London—why not remain in Transylvania?

DRACULA: Ah, my friend, there is a reason—and did you but see with my eyes and know with my knowledge you would perhaps better understand.

[MISS MORRIS *enters quickly with parcel under her arm.*]

MORRIS: Here we are, Professor—I've got the goods! Just caught your friend Vanderpool as he was leaving his place. Seemed rather astonished at the amount of stuff you ordered, but said, as it was you, he guessed it was all right.

VAN HELSING: Thank you my friend—you have indeed been speedy. Permit me.

[*He takes knife from pocket and cuts string of parcel, and in doing so cuts himself.*]

MORRIS: Oh, Professor! You've cut yourself!

VAN HELSING: It is nothing—a scratch. [*To* DRACULA.] See?

DRACULA: Take care—take care how you cut yourself—it is more dangerous than you think!

VAN HELSING: [*On opening parcel glances at* DRACULA.] Would it be of interest to you to see what I have prescribed for Madame?

DRACULA: [*Crossing to table.*] Any steps you take to alleviate the malady of our charming hostess are of the *deepest* interest to me.

VAN HELSING: See here, then—

[VAN HELSING *plunges his hand into the parcel and draws out a handful of withered, whitish flowers. These he thrusts forward to the Count and watches keenly the effect on him.* DRACULA *stands transfixed, then an expression of blind, ungovernable rage comes over his face, and putting out both hands as though to ward off the smell of the flowers—backs toward the centre door speaking as he goes.*]

DRACULA: Have care, Van Helsing! This is a joke that you'll repent! These noxious flowers! An outrage! An outrage, I say! If you think you can—! [*Suddenly his rage leaves him, and smiling slightly as he opens the door, he continues in a suave, courteous manner.*] I live too long in Italy to care for the smell of garlic. Perhaps you will be good enough to excuse me.

[DRACULA *exits. As the door closes,* VAN HELSING *and* MISS

Miss Morris's uncanny ability to make a return trip from suburban Hampstead to central London's Soho in the space of a few minutes implies that she, too, might be possessed of distinctly supernatural talents.

MORRIS *look at each other. Then* VAN HELSING *stares straight in front of him, and draws in his breath with a sharp hiss.*]

VAN HELSING: So-o-o!

MORRIS: Our friend doesn't seem to care for garlic! If he goes up in the air over a trivial thing like that, I'm not crazy to really annoy him!

VAN HELSING: Perhaps my friend, it is not to *him* so trivial a thing — we shall see!

MORRIS: Well, sometimes — way back home — I've caught a whiff of garlic, from some "Dago" or "Mex" in the subway — but I never "saw red" like the Count, just now — that's got me beat!

VAN HELSING: Would you be so good as to ask Dr. Seward and Mr. Harker to come to me here — and bring with them Madame Mina. If she sleeps, wake her — she must come!

MORRIS: Why certainly, Professor! [*Exit.*]

[MORRIS *exits.* VAN HELSING *stands centre of stage — thinks for a moment — then, taking in the position of the Chesterfield — he crosses to it and arranges cushions on left arm, then turns right and left in turn, taking in the position of the doors, furniture, etc. Finally he crosses to extreme right up stage*

"I live too long in Italy to care for the smell of garlic." Van Helsing proves the wisdom of an old folk remedy. Caricature by Tom Titt.

and draws the attention of the audience to electric light switch — by switching off all lights, except from fire. He moves into firelight and takes in the fact that right across the room, the firelight plays dimly on the couch. Apparently satisfied, he switches on lights again, as the centre door opens and MINA, SEWARD, HARKER *and then* MORRIS *enter.*]

VAN HELSING: [*Moving forward to* MINA.] Ah, Madame, I fear you have been talking — and I caution you not to fatigue yourself. [*Taking her arm and leading her towards couch.*] Is it not that you rest here awhile, I have a little business to discuss with our friends here. [MINA *lies full length on couch, and* VAN HELSING *arranges cushions under her head, so that when lights go out, the face and neck are clearly defined in the firelight. He stands and looks keenly at the group of men round the couch.*] Where is Lord Godalming? I have need of him, also friend John — perhaps you will be so kind as to ask him to come to us, in the Hall — at once — *now*.

SEWARD: Certainly. [*Exits.*]

VAN HELSING: And now Madame you will think it strange our leaving you, when I gave so strict orders to the contrary — but please be of belief that what I do, I do of purpose — and for your good, Madame.

MINA: I am certain of that Professor. I only hope I shan't fall asleep. I can stand anything but those awful dreams.

VAN HELSING: [*Indicating that they leave.*] Now, gentlemen!

"For an instant my heart stood still." Raymond Huntley and Dora Mary Patrick.

[VAN HELSING *switches off lights. Before* HARKER *leaves he crosses to couch, and bending over, he touches his wife's hair with his lips. The others go quietly out.* VAN HELSING *waits at door for* HARKER. *Then, after a quick look round the room, he goes out last, closing the folding doors.*

[*At least 20 seconds elapse. No movement of any kind.*

[*Then* MINA *gives a slight start, but settles down again and closes her eyes.*

[*Twelve seconds elapse.*

[*Then, from the door right,* DRACULA *enters — sees* MINA — *crosses slowly towards her.*]

DRACULA: At last, Madame, I have the pleasure of seeing you alone.

[*He stands at head of couch smiling down at her — she gives a piercing in-drawn scream. The folding doors open and in a blaze of light you see* VAN HELSING, GODALMING, HARKER *and* MISS MORRIS — *who hold the picture for a moment then rush down to the couch. The instant the blaze of light hits the eyes of the audience* DRACULA *slips behind couch and out through scene trap. As the men come down they all speak following lines* together — *and hold, without movement, their positions round the couch.* MISS MORRIS *switches on lights.*]

VAN HELSING: You are all right, Madame?

SEWARD: God! What was that?

HARKER: Mina — speak to me!

GODALMING: We shouldn't have left her.

MORRIS: Who switched these lights?

[*Having spoken all together they make no further sound or movement at all.* DRACULA *enters quietly through folding doors.*]

DRACULA: And how is the patient now? Better — I hope!

CURTAIN

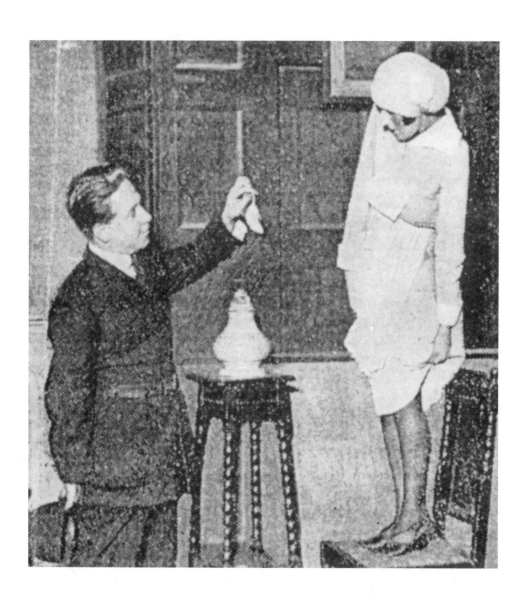

Act Two

Scene: MINA'*s boudoir.*

A prettily furnished room with bedroom leading off upstage, at back left. Window in boudoir, upstage at back right, entrance door in flat, upper left. Table right centre. Sofa down left, fireplace right.

As curtain rises, the HOUSEMAID *enters from bedroom, switching off the lights; she crosses to fireplace and is just bending down to attend to the fire, when there is a knock at the boudoir door, and the head of a man in Warder's uniform comes round the corner.*

MAID: Good Lord, you gave me a start. What do you want here, anyway?

WARDER: Excuse me, miss, but you don't 'appen to have seen anything of our guvnor's pet loonie? He's out again, he is!

MAID: Look 'ere, either that blessed Lunatic Asylum of yours will have to move, or I will, I can't stand it much longer. I'm scared stiff, what with foreign counts appearing from nowhere, lunatics howling, doors opening and shutting for no reason. I'm getting fair jumpy, and now there is a new horror, this 'ere Dutch Sherlock Holmes with the X-ray eyes!

WARDER: What d'yer mean, "X-ray eyes"?

MAID: I mean what I say. When that bloke looks at you — I'll swear he sees clean through you, that's X-ray isn't it?

WARDER: You'll have to live on Bismuth, that's the only thing X-rays can't get through; but I'm asking you, 'ave you seen my loonie, or 'aven't you?

MAID: 'Course I 'aven't, besides what would he be doing in 'ere?

WARDER: Lord knows, but I got to his cell door, just in time to see his legs disappearing through the window; time I got to the window, he was capering towards this 'ouse for all he was worth, he made for the front door.

According to cast member Ivan Butler, this bantering scene was sometimes deleted to shorten the play sufficiently to permit two evening performances — a testament to the play's popularity, but a grueling ordeal for the actors.

Opposite: Rats were taboo on stage, so a white mouse was called into service to provide laughs instead of chills. Jack Howarth (left) played the warden and Betty Murgatroyd (right) played the housemaid in the Little Theatre production.

MAID: Lord bless us and save us—send for the police!

WARDER: Police, 'nothing; takes a man my size to deal with these chaps, they're scared stiff of me, they are. But you needn't be afraid of this bloke, he's quite 'armless.

MAID: You sure he is?

WARDER: Certain, why he wouldn't 'urt a fly—'e only eats 'em.

MAID: Eats flies! Go on!

WARDER: I ain't joking, why 'e'd rather eat a few bluebottles than a pound of best steak, any day, and what 'e does to spiders is a crime.

MAID: Spiders!

WARDER: Yes—'e feeds 'em to a couple of sparrows 'e's got. Yesterday 'e wanted the guvnor to give 'im a kitten; I don't know what eats cats, but that don't matter, it's when 'e gets on to something that *I* can eat, I'm watching 'im.

MAID: Seems to me, somebody'll be coming after *you* in a minute. You and your spiders!

WARDER: All right, 'ave it yer own way—but this is a queer neighbourhood—don't you never feel a bit lonesome like, going up and down this avenue on your nights off?

MAID: Just lately I 'ave a bit; I never noticed the trees 'ad such shadows before!

WARDER: Well—er—er—ahem! If you feel you'd like a h'escort, Miss, I'm yours to command—as Daphne Du Maurier says!

MAID: All right, but don't come in your uniform, people might think I'm barmy!

WARDER: Good egg! It's a bargain—shall we say tomorrow?

MAID: Very well—tomorrow at eight. I say you haven't wasted much time—'ave you?

WARDER: Well, you see, Miss, I've had my eyes on you for some time—besides they tell me I'm the swiftest worker in London.

MAID: Oh, you go on! You hate yourself, don't you?

WARDER: Well—the doctor says I'm very "self-respecting" and I'm not sure—

MAID: 'Ere you buzz off, and find your lunatics elsewhere—the missus'll be coming up directly.

WARDER: All right—suppose I'll 'ave to tempt 'im back to his cell—lucky I've got a "tit-bit" for 'im.

MAID: Why, what's that?

[WARDER *puts his hand in pocket and takes out a white mouse by the tail.* MAID *screams loudly.*] You little beast! Look 'ere,

In productions of Dracula, *maids are always well-attuned to horror. Caricature by E.S. Hynes.*

that appointment for tomorrow night is off—see, right
off!

WARDER: Well—well—some people 'as no sense of humour. You
must watch your step on that avenue tomorrow night. [*He shudders
violently and goes out.*]

MAID: Well of all the . . . Nice cheery little thing 'e'd be to 'ave about
the house.

[*She goes toward the door, as she gets there it opens and* VAN
HELSING *and* SEWARD *come in quickly—the former carrying
his parcel of garlic, which he places on table right centre. The*
MAID *stands back to let them enter, then goes out quietly, closing
door behind her.*]

SEWARD: What did you make of that, Van Helsing?

VAN HELSING: It is precisely as I thought. Perhaps, my friend, you are
more inclined to believe now?

SEWARD: As we opened the door there was undoubtedly a figure
bending over the couch—but whose? And where did it disappear?

VAN HELSING: I know no more—or very little more than you—it was
the figure of a man—but the face I saw not, and only have my
suspicion.

SEWARD: Tell me, Van Helsing—on whom do your suspicions rest?
Do you connect whoever it is with Mina's illness?

VAN HELSING: Most assuredly I do—besides did you not hear
Madame say just now: "The same red eyes—the same white
face"?

SEWARD: But don't you think it possible that she may have dozed
off—and have been dreaming?

VAN HELSING: Dreaming! When we ourselves saw precisely what she
saw—we could not all have been dreaming!

SEWARD: Tell me, Van Helsing—who is it you suspect?

VAN HELSING: Well, my friend, I know it will be of difficulty for you
to believe, and in the absence of proof, perhaps I should not speak;
but I am not satisfied in my mind as to the Count Dracula—I have
observed certain things about him.

SEWARD: Such as?

VAN HELSING: He shows no reflection in a mirror, and his abnormal
detestation of these so harmless little flowers—all point to one
thing!

From the notice in *The
Era*: "The incredible thing
is that nobody connected
the illness with Count Dracula before Van Helsing arrived. The sight alone of
this terrible waxen creature
from Transylvania would
have made most of us ill,
but the family doctor—the
stupidest person we have
seen in a play for a long
time—had the shock of his
life when his friend, Van
Helsing, diagnosed Dracula
as the evil cause of the
trouble."

SEWARD: And do you mean to tell me that you consider that man directly responsible for the death of Lucy, and the present illness of Mina?

VAN HELSING: My friend, until I have "proof" I can only *suspect*. It was in order to obtain proof that I left Madame Mina "unguarded" just now, and but for the rapid disappearance of this "man-that-was", we should all have known.

SEWARD: You laid a trap for him?

VAN HELSING: Precisely. To this type of "un-dead," the blood is the life — and blood he must have! Only a few minutes ago in the study he became aware that through the medium of these garlic flowers I proposed to render access to his victims impossible. He therefore seized the first opportunity to approach her.

SEWARD: And what do you propose to do now?

VAN HELSING: I must *know* positively from whence this danger comes — to that end I would wish to acquaint our friends downstairs with all I know, and all I suspect. We shall need — of help — every atom we can obtain.

SEWARD: And Mina herself?

VAN HELSING: She must be told too — but not yet — I fear the shock for her will be very great!

SEWARD: Shall I bring the others here now?

VAN HELSING: If you will be so good — one moment — you will bring Harker and Miss Morris here, but Lord Godalming you will leave with Madame — with strict injunctions not to leave her for a moment. Him, we will acquaint afterwards. Meantime, with my little flowers, I will render this room safe for Madame.

SEWARD: Right! I'll bring them here in a minute.

> [*Exits. Directly* DR. SEWARD *has gone,* VAN HELSING *draws the curtain of the bedroom window and latches window securely. Then, taking a handful of garlic flowers, he rubs them all over the sashes. He then does the same thing with door and fireplace. As he moves towards the boudoir there is a knock at the door and* SEWARD *enters followed by* HARKER *and* MISS MORRIS.]

VAN HELSING: Ah! My friends — and how is Madame now?

HARKER: She seems to have pretty nearly got over her fright — but tell me, Professor, what *does* all this mean?

VAN HELSING: My friends, I have much of importance to tell you — but first of all I would ask you to try and keep an "open mind" — for what I shall say will seem to you "impossible" — but later you shall find it is only too true. The death of poor Miss Lucy—and the present illness of Madame Mina—is caused by a "Were-Wolf" or "Vampire"—

HARKER: A Vampire! Professor, how can you expect us to believe a thing like that?

VAN HELSING: Wait, my friend. I have learned not to think lightly of anyone's belief no matter how strange it be—for your own sake and for hers—at least let me finish what I have to say. There are such beings as Vampires, the teachings and the records of the past give proof enough for sane peoples. I admit that at first I was skeptic—but had I known at the first what I know now—and had I only been here—one so precious life had been spared to many of you who did love her. But that is past and we must so work that other poor souls perish not. The Vampire does not die—like the bee when he sting once—he is only stronger, and being so, have yet more power to work evil. This vampire which is amongst us is of himself so strong as twenty men, he is of cunning more than mortal, for his cunning be the growth of ages. He is brute, and more than brute, and the heart of him is not. He cannot die by mere passing of time. So long as he can fatten on the blood of the living, he can grow even younger. He can transform himself at will to any of the forms of the meaner things, such as the rat—the bat—the wolf. He can come in mist which he creates, or in moonlight rays, as elemental dust. He can vanish at will. He can see in the dark. He can do all these things—and yet he is not free. His power ceases, as does that of all evil things, at the coming of the day—he can only change himself at his change time—at moon, or at exact sunrise or sunset. Then there are things which so afflict him that he has no power, as the garlic here, and as for things sacred, at the sight of the crucifix he takes his place off— and silent with respect. Our only chance of dealing with that "man-that-was" is to waste not a moment in finding his "earth-home" and at his weakest moment—sunset—to destroy him. Life is nothing, I heed him not—for if we fail and this vampire conquers, it is not mere life and death—it is that we become as himself, foul things of the night, without heart or conscience. But we are face to face with duty. Shall we shrink from it—what say you?

HARKER: I answer for Mina and myself.

MORRIS: Well, I guess I'm handicapped, being only a girl—but I can keep my end up—so count me in, Professor!

Sam Livesey as Van Helsing. Caricature by E.S. Hynes.

SEWARD: You know how I stand, Van Helsing, and I'm dead certain of Godalming.

VAN HELSING: That is good. We shall have to pass through the bitter water before we reach the sweet. Well, you know now what we have to contend against; all we have to go upon are tradition and supersition, but we have on our side, power of "combination"—a power denied to the vampire kind, and we have the resources of science.

HARKER: And do you mean to say, Professor, that you believe this vampire to be actually amongst us now?

VAN HELSING: I am certain of it.

MORRIS: Then in Heaven's name, Professor—tell us straight out whom do you believe it to be.

VAN HELSING: [*Looking carefully round room before speaking.*] I strongly suspect—but as yet have no actual proof—that it is your guest—the Count Dracula!

MORRIS: Dracula!

HARKER: Oh, my God! And to think that I was instrumental in bringing that beast to London.

VAN HELSING: You cannot blame yourself for that. London with its millions has doubtless been his goal for years past—and come he would have, some way, somehow!

HARKER: What in Heaven's name are we going to do?

VAN HELSING: We must in all things move cautiously, but swiftly—once we have made certain he is the author of these crimes, we shall not waste a moment in dealing with him.

HARKER: Why not go straight to the police?

VAN HELSING: My friend, that would be worse than useless—what Inspector at your Scotland Yard would listen for one moment to this apparently "Cock-and-Bull" story?

MORRIS: But surely, Professor, if *you* believe in the existence of these vampires there must be some men of science at the Yard who would at least admit the possibility of the thing, and take the matter up—from that point of view?

VAN HELSING: Well—that is why I asked to see you all here—to tell you plainly what I suspect and to ascertain what you wish to do. It concerns you principally, Mr. Harker—and so if it is your wish to inform the police—! [*He shrugs his shoulders.*]

HARKER: Professor, this is all so new to me—I haven't had time even to think as yet. Just tell us—what definite reasons have you for *not* wishing to call in the police?

Moira Lynd as Quincy Morris.

VAN HELSING: Well, firstly as I said, they would flatly disbelieve and, secondly, that no power on earth could prevent this Vampire from slipping through their fingers — dissolving into thin air — no matter how closely guarded and confined he was — and starting operations elsewhere!

SEWARD: Well, if I may be allowed to say so, if you fellows had known Van Helsing as long as I have, you would be guided entirely by him and do what he suggests — without question.

VAN HELSING: I should not say that, friend John. I am by no means infallible — it is possible that I have even made a wrong diagnosis of this case, but I am prepared to stake my professional reputation that I have not.

HARKER: And are you equally certain that this Count Dracula is to blame?

VAN HELSING: No, I am not — I only *suspect!* Remember, I have been in this house but a few hours — in that time I have made certain "tests" — and I am not satisfied. But soon, very soon, I shall know for certain.

HARKER: And then — ?

VAN HELSING: And then we shall have to take the matter of the "removal" of this "undead" thing into our own hands, and the responsibility will be great and the risk greater. But in my opinion it is the only way.

MORRIS: I am with *you*, Professor.

SEWARD: There is no doubt in my mind — and never has been.

HARKER: Van Helsing — you must go your own way — I am entirely in your hands.

[VAN HELSING *nods.*]

But tell me, Professor, what do you intend to do about my wife?

VAN HELSING: Madame is ill — very ill — but it is only through heavy loss of blood. I understand there has been a transfusion yesterday morning — and there shall be more.

MORRIS: Well, I don't think you'll have far to go to find "volunteers" — I — for one, am entirely at her service.

SEWARD: And I!

HARKER: I think you know how I feel about it, Professor!

VAN HELSING: Good! Now there is no occasion to keep Madame out of her room any longer. We shall if we may, Mr. Harker, go down to your lounge where I would wish to discuss some further details, and arrange our plan of action; besides Lord Godalming must be

The housemaid ponders the relationship of the human and animal worlds.

told — but I would most *strongly impress upon you*, that outside of we five people — no living soul must have even a hint as to what we suspect about Count Dracula!

> [*A yell of maniac laughter is heard from the boudoir window, that still has its curtains drawn. The men stand rigid and silent for a moment, then* HARKER *and* SEWARD *rush to the curtains and draw them back, revealing the figure of a man of medium height, with a white face, who is leaning back against the window with arms folded, and is still laughing. A second's pause, then* SEWARD *speaks.*]

SEWARD: Renfield! What in thunder are you doing here?

RENFIELD: [*Coming down stage.*] Lord! What fools we mortals are! [*Laughs again.*]

SEWARD: I asked you, Renfield, what are you doing here?

RENFIELD: [*Quietly.*] I wanted particularly to see you, Dr. Seward.

SEWARD: You know quite well I have done my rounds for tonight; you can see me in the morning.

RENFIELD: But it's vitally important I should see you now.

> [*The three men look at each other hopelessly perplexed as to what to do.* VAN HELSING *makes a signal to* DR. SEWARD.]

SEWARD: Renfield! You overheard what we were talking about?

RENFIELD: Oh, yes — I heard!

SEWARD: And how much of it did you understand?

RENFIELD: I understood enough to know that this gentleman [*Indicating* VAN HELSING.] knows more of what he is talking about than all the rest of you put together — and if you are only guided by him —

> [*There is a dull thud on the window pane — the curtains are now fully opened and a large bat is seen flapping its wings against the glass, evidently attracted by the light. The men turn quickly to the window, but seeing what has caused the noise, pay no further attention. The effect on* RENFIELD, *however, is electrical; he stops short in his speech, stares at the window, becomes confused and goes on hurriedly.*]

Of course I heard you talking, but I don't know what on earth it was all about — such things are of no interest to me!

SEWARD: [*To* VAN HELSING.] He did hear — but memory is not one of his strong points. Besides he sees no one but the warders — and they are not likely to listen to anything he says.

For Harry Ludlam's 1962 book *A Biography of Dracula: The Life Story of Bram Stoker*, company member Ivan Butler recalled some of the ingenious stage effects created for Hamilton Deane's production. Renfield's weird cries, along with the howling of wolves, were accomplished with the aid of an off-stage megaphone. "For Dracula's weird 'wail' call we used either a violin or a swannee whistle. The bat which tried to fly in through the windows was an ingenious affair of black cloth and wire about eighteen inches across with the wings spread, its glowing red eyes lit up by a torch battery fixed in the body. It was operated by the assistant stage manager, who used to stand on a chair outside the windows using a sort of fishing rod to swing the bat around. On one famous occasion when the string broke, the bat sailed in through the window and landed in the footlights, where it stayed glaring unwinkingly out at the audience. As this was supposed to be Dracula in one of his guises, it tended to make his eventual entry a little difficult."

RENFIELD: Fools! Fools! You too, Doctor, whom I always looked upon as being wise!

SEWARD: What on earth do you mean?

[*There is a moment's pause then* VAN HELSING *goes straight to* RENFIELD *taking him by the shoulders.*]

VAN HELSING: What do you know of Count Dracula?

RENFIELD: Count Dracula! [*Is just going to speak — looks towards window then grins foolishly.*] What should I know of Count Dracula? I've never heard the name before. Besides [*Drawing himself up to* SEWARD.] Mr. . . . Mr. . . . You have the advantage of me. Excuse me, Doctor, but you haven't introduced me to your friends.

SEWARD: Well — really, Renfield!

Bernard Jukes as the memorable, maniacal Renfield.

VAN HELSING: Humour him — do so!

SEWARD: Oh, well! Miss Morris, Mr. Harker, Professor Van Helsing . . . Mr. Renfield — a patient of mine!

RENFIELD: [*Shaking hands with each in turn — stops opposite* VAN HELSING.] Ah! Who has not heard of Van Helsing — the man who has revolutionised therapeutics by his discovery of the continuous evolution of brain matter, and who has, if I make no mistake, more than a slight knowledge of the occult — which may prove useful to all of you at this moment. Now, gentlemen, I call you to witness that I am at least as sane as the majority of men who are in full possession of their liberty. Dr. Seward, I desire to go now — at once — this very moment if I may; I am asking this not on personal grounds—but for the sake of others!

[SEWARD *moves forward to speak but* VAN HELSING *touches his arm.*]

VAN HELSING: Can you tell us frankly your real reason for wishing to be free tonight?

RENFIELD: I cannot. If I were to tell you that, you would all be convinced that I am mad—and I'm not—I'm not!

VAN HELSING: Well, Mr. Renfield, at least you can tell me this—if you are able to escape from your quarters and to enter this room, why not escape altogether? Why wait the permission of our good doctor here?

RENFIELD: Sometimes wise men are fools and we who are kept in padded cells are wise. I have a mission to perform here before I go—that's what has brought me here tonight. But can't you see, man, that I am as logical and as sane as you?

VAN HELSING: I begin to believe you, Renfield!

SEWARD: [*To* VAN HELSING.] Leave him to me a moment. Well, Renfield, what about the flies these days?

RENFIELD: The fly, my dear sir, has one striking feature—its wings are typical of the aerial powers of the psychic faculties. The ancients did well—when they typified the soul as a butterfly!

SEWARD: Oh, it's a soul you are after now—is it?

RENFIELD: Oh, no—oh, no—I want no souls. Life is all I want—and blood is the life! Life is a positive and perpetual entity, and by consuming a multitude of live things—no matter how low in the scale of creation—one may indefinitely prolong life. But I don't want any souls . . . indeed I don't . . . they would be no use to me . . . I couldn't eat them or—

SEWARD: But how are you to get the life, without getting the soul also? [RENFIELD *looks puzzled.*] A nice time you'll have some day when you are flying out there, with the souls of thousands of flies and spiders, and birds and cats, buzzing and twittering and miauing all round you. You've got their lives, you know—and you must put up with their souls!

[RENFIELD *puts his fingers in his ears, and shuts his eyes, screwing them up tightly.*]

RENFIELD: To hell with you and your souls! Why do you plague me about souls? Haven't I got enough to worry and distract me already without thinking of souls!

Audiences at the Little Theatre were greeted by a uniformed nurse who dispensed smelling salts to audience members incapacitated by shock. The gimmick was first introduced to London audiences a few seasons earlier when Sybil Thorndike presented her season of English Grand Guignol in the same playhouse. Harry Ludlam, in his book *A Biography of Dracula*, reported that during each performance "at times calculated to coincide with horrible goings-on on stage, she walked slowly and quietly down the aisles, hovering within vision of quaking customers." According to Ludlam, she revived an average of seven patients a night, and on one memorable evening, attended to "the wholesale collapse of no fewer than twenty-nine people."

SEWARD: Renfield!

RENFIELD: Forgive me, Doctor, I forgot myself! I am so worried in my mind that I am apt to be irritable. If you only knew the problem I have to face, you would pity and pardon me. Please don't put me in a strait-jacket. I want to think, and I can't think freely when my body is confined!

SEWARD: Well, come now—wouldn't you like some sugar to spread out for your flies?

RENFIELD: Flies! [*A look of animation comes over his face—then passes.*] Oh, flies are but poor things! [*As he speaks, he follows with his eyes an imaginary fly which settles near him. With a sweep of his hand he catches it and an exultant look comes into his face—then seeing the other men watching him, he releases it quickly.*] Bother them all! I don't care a pin about them now! The Master is at hand!

VAN HELSING: [*Quickly.*] Master! What Master?

Renfield's diet craze: small lives, with blood in them.

RENFIELD: What's that to do with you? I wish you'd take yourself and your idiotic brain theories somewhere else! Damn all thick-headed Dutchmen! [*Turning and clasping* DR. SEWARD.] Doctor, for God's sake, let me out of this house at once. Send me away how and where you will, let them take me in a strait-jacket, manacled, even to a gaol, but let me go out of this. You don't know what you do by keeping me here. You don't know whom you wrong or how, and I may not tell! By all you hold sacred, for the sake of the Almighty, save my soul from guilt. The Master has come and he is calling me; calling, I say, and I dare not disobey. But I don't want to be like him! Help me to save my immortal soul. Let me go!

SEWARD: [*Raising him up.*] Come no more of this! We have had quite enough already. Get to your bed!

RENFIELD: [*Rising—stands facing* SEWARD *for a few seconds, then very quietly says:*] You will—I trust, Doctor—bear in mind, in view of what may happen, that I did what I could to convince you tonight.

[*A knock is heard on boudoir door, and* GODALMING's *voice asking if they may come in.* MINA *and* GODALMING *enter—the former stands facing* RENFIELD.]

RENFIELD: Are you Mrs. Harker?

MINA: I am.

RENFIELD: Then you are the lady I delayed my escape to see tonight!

MINA: What do you want with me?

RENFIELD: Madame—as you value your life—by your hope of the hereafter—I beg of you to leave this place—now—at once!

MINA: But why, Mr. Renfield? This is my home!

RENFIELD: Home or not, I beg of you to at least put running water between you and this place. Oh, I know I am looked upon here simply as Dr. Seward's pet lunatic, but I'm not so mad as not to know positively that if you remain here it means death and worse than death to you—Oh, please, Madame—believe me and go!

MINA: [*Appealing to the others.*] What does he mean?

SEWARD: My patient is a little over-wrought tonight. Come with me at once, Renfield—we'll have no more of this nonsense!

MINA: I thank you, Mr. Renfield, for what appears to be a good intention!

RENFIELD: Mrs. Harker, you and your friends here will bitterly regret not accepting my warning. I tell you—you are in the power of—[*There is a decided crash and rattle of the window panes. Instantly* RENFIELD'*s manner changes—he rushes towards the window and cringes abjectly. Speaking through window:*] Oh, Master, Master! I told them nothing—I told them nothing—I am loyal—I am your slave!

VAN HELSING: Quick! What does he see?

> [SEWARD *takes* RENFIELD'*s arm and leads him away.* GOD-ALMING *and* MISS MORRIS *draw curtains and look out.*]

MORRIS: Say, there's nothing there but a big bat, flying in a circle—

GODALMING: [*Pointing down towards ground.*] It looks like a large grey dog—see it now, Miss Morris, just passing that small shrub?

> [*Exit* MISS MORRIS *quietly—boudoir door.*]

VAN HELSING: Are you sure it is a dog?

GODALMING: Well it might easily be a wo— Oh, but that's nonsense—it's a dog, right enough!

SEWARD: Come with me, Renfield.

RENFIELD: [*In state of abject fear.*] Doctor, would you allow one of your friends to go with us across the lawn to my cell?

GODALMING: I'll go—with pleasure—but what's the idea?

RENFIELD: As the Doctor has told you, I am perhaps a little "over-wrought" tonight. Goodbye, Mrs. Harker. Since you will not accept my warning, I pray God I may never see your face again. May He bless you and keep you. [*To* SEWARD.] Don't tie me, please. [*Raises his right hand, pointing first two fingers at her, then with a quick look towards boudoir window he goes out, followed by* SEWARD *and* GODALMING. VAN HELSING *and* HARKER *stand watching him go.* MINA

Members of Hamilton Deane's Dracula *company, in Bradford, Yorkshire, in 1929. At left, W.E. Holloway, who played the role of Dracula. (Courtesy of Ivan Butler)*

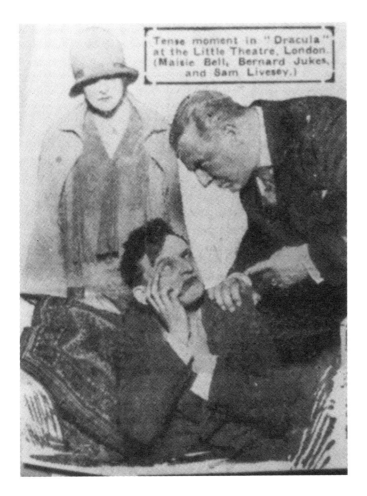

Tense moment in "Dracula" at the Little Theatre, London. (Maisie Bell, Bernard Jukes, and Sam Livesey.)

"Dracula? I've never heard the name before."

is seated on couch.]

HARKER: Well, Professor, if that man wasn't "bluffing" he is about the sanest lunatic I ever saw. I believe he had some serious purpose in coming here, and if he had it was pretty rough on him not to get a chance. But why the extraordinary interest in Mina here?

MINA: Poor man, I'm certain he means well. He seems well—he seems to think I am in danger from some unknown quarter. But of course it's only part of his madness.

[VAN HELSING *and* HARKER *exchange a meaning glance.*]

VAN HELSING: I have made my specialty the brain, but it is a new experience to me to find a lunatic who talks philosophy, and reasons so soundly. Mental disease is a fascinating study—

Moira Lynd was a pistol-packing Quincey Morris when Deane's play moved to the Prince of Wales Theatre.

perhaps I may gain more knowledge out of the folly of this madman than I shall from the teaching of the most wise.

[*A revolver shot is heard outside.* MINA *stands bolt upright—* HARKER *goes to her.* VAN HELSING *pulls curtains aside and looks out.*]

HARKER: What was that?

VAN HELSING: I do not know, but Miss Morris is running across the lawn towards the house. Come, Madame, there is nothing to be alarmed at, we shall know the why of it in a moment.

HARKER: Did she fire or was she fired at, I wonder?

MORRIS: [*Enters quickly and rather breathlessly.*] Say, I'm most awfully sorry to throw a scare into you, but the fact is that I've got such a horror of bats that I can't stand them, so I ran out and had a shot at it.

VAN HELSING: Did you hit it?

MORRIS: I fancy not, for it flew away towards the wood.

MINA: Why do you hate bats so much, dear?

MORRIS: Well, partly from recent events and partly because years ago, when I was visiting some friends of mine, on the Pampas, one of those "vampire bats" got hold of a favourite mare of mine—and the next morning she was too weak from loss of blood to stand up and I had to have her shot.

VAN HELSING: Come, come, Madame Mina, you must not let your mind dwell on these things—see here, these are for you. [*Picking up double handful of garlic.*] They are medicinal, but you do not know. I put him in your window. I hang him round your neck—so that you sleep well. Oh, yes—they like the lotus flower, make your trouble forgotten.

MINA: [*Picking up flowers. Smells them and throws them down.*] Oh, Professor, you must be joking—these are only dried garlic.

VAN HELSING: Madame Mina, I do not jest. There is a grim purpose in what I do—there is much virtue in these so common flowers. Friend Harker, you will rub this handful round this window here, and particularly above the sashes. See, Madame, I make myself the necklace you will wear tonight.

MINA: Professor, anyone would think that you were working some spell to keep out an evil spirit.

VAN HELSING: Perhaps I am, Madame! Now—are you ready? [*He gently fixes the flowers round her neck in the form of a rough necklace.*] Take care you do not disturb or remove this and even if the room feel close, do not — on any account — open the window or the door once you have retired for the night.

MINA: I promise — and thank you a thousand times for all your kindness and care for me.

VAN HELSING: And now, good night, Madame — you will not mind my taking friend husband away with me just a few minutes, there are some matters we must discuss — and meantime I will send your maid to you. God send you a peaceful night untroubled by those "dreams" you spoke of. Now, my friends, will you come with me?

MORRIS: Good night, Mina dear. [*Kisses her.*] Remember, you are surrounded by your friends.

HARKER: I don't like leaving you, dear, but the Professor considers it safe and he needs me. I'll be back as soon as I can.

[*They go out,* MORRIS *first, then* HARKER, *then* VAN HELSING, *who takes a quick look round room.*]

[*After they have gone,* MINA *stands centre for a moment, fingering her necklace of flowers, picks up scarf from chair right, switches off the lights, then turns as though to go to bedroom. The door leading to bedroom flies open — then shuts again of its own accord. As she gets to door, she draws back with a little gasp and puts out her hands, coming slowly downstage backwards. She turns, holding her hands to her head. There is a sharp knock at the door.* MINA *starts, but before she can say "Come in" the* MAID *enters quickly, sees there is something wrong with her mistress. Putting her arm round her she leads her gently to couch left, switches on table lamp above couch, saying as she does so:*]

"No wonder you are feeling faint, Madame, with those awful smelling flowers ..." Caricature by Tom Titt.

MAID: You are not feeling well, Madame — lean on me.

[*She places* MINA *on couch, then looks round for smelling salts — gets them — offers them to* MINA *— notices garlic.*]

No wonder you are feeling faint, Madame, with those awful smelling flowers round your neck. [*She unties flowers — they drop to floor.*]

MINA: No — no — the Professor said ...

MAID: [*Looking towards window.*] Why, the window is shut, Madame — may I open it?

[*She crosses — draws curtains — screams — draws back. As she leaves window with curtain open the audience distinctly sees in*

Deane intended to employ
considerably more blood-
and-thunder leading up to
the second act curtain, but
was vetoed by the Lord
Chamberlain. "Mina, left
alone—rises to draw the
curtains, as she does so—
there is a 'crash'—the
whole window falls in, and
the head and shoulders of a
large grey wolf [are] seen
against the bright moon-
light—remains a second,
then withdraws—and a
steady stream of smoke
rushes through the broken
pane. Mina gives a piercing
scream, and falls in a dead
faint." Following a brief
curtain, "a dense 'pall' of
'smoke' or 'mist'" covers
the window, "through which
is seen the face and form of
Dracula heading toward the
figure on the floor." With
or without the Lord Cham-
berlain's approval, Deane
evidently reinstated some of
this material: in its review
of the London production,
The Era explicitly de-
scribed "the sickening picture of Dracula coming out
of a fog and fastening his
teeth on the victim's
throat."

*the moonlight the form of a huge bat which thuds and flutters
against the glass—then disappears.*]

MINA: Ask my husband to come to me at once—he is in the study.
MAID: I don't like leaving you, Madame.
MINA: Go quickly—

[*Exit* MAID, *looking over shoulder.* MINA, *left alone, rises to
draw the curtains. As she does so, there is a heavy "thud" at the
window—the pane of glass is broken and through the aperture
thus made creeps in a stream of smoke, whilst outside the
window she sees the face of* DRACULA.]

THE CURTAIN FALLS

Act Three

Study as in Act I. Afternoon — three days later.

As curtain rises, SEWARD *is discovered seated on couch oiling a small revolver. He replaces oil on mantelpiece and then carefully inserts cartridges into gun; examines each before doing so. As folding doors open, he puts revolver in his pocket.*

VAN HELSING *enters — he looks carefully round room.*

SEWARD: Any change?

VAN HELSING: Worse — decidedly worse! Ever since that night when Dracula broke through my "garlic defences" and Harker found his wife in a dead faint — with the little wounds in her throat — freshly re-opened, she seems to have lost even the desire to live.

SEWARD: Are you certain, Van Helsing, that since that night he has not managed to get at her again?

VAN HELSING: Positively — for one moment she has not been left unguarded, besides, the Count knows now that we suspect him — and in consequence is very wary. But friend John, there is something that you and I must talk of alone — later we may have to take the others into our confidence. Our poor dear Madame Mina is "changing".

SEWARD: My God, Van Helsing — what do you mean?

VAN HELSING: I can see the characteristics of the Vampire coming in her face. It is now but very slight — but it is to be seen — her teeth are somewhat sharper, and at times her eyes are more hard, but these are not all — there is to her the "Silence" now — often — and that is the worst sign.

SEWARD: What if these symptoms develop further?

VAN HELSING: They cannot develop much further because the instant the Vampire dies, his power over her is gone, forever — and die he shall — tonight at sunset!

SEWARD: All arrangements have been made — there is only the question of which earth-box we shall find him in now; and at this moment Harker and Morris are seeing to that.

VAN HELSING: One other thing you must know. Whether tonight we make this Vampire "true-dead" or not, Miss Lucy remains "undead" and unless we adopt the same course as we take with him — she will carry on the work, which he shall have left unfinished.

SEWARD: But do you suppose Lord Godalming would ever consent to your doing this thing?

VAN HELSING: I shall tell him and try hard to obtain his full consent but whether he consents or not — for the sake of humanity in general it shall be done. But tell me, have you seen your patient this morning?

SEWARD: I visit him often — but he's never twice alike — one moment humming a tune — the next he is moody and sullen.

VAN HELSING: Has he got over your refusal to let him go?

SEWARD: No — it seems to be on his mind. If that man had been an ordinary lunatic I would have trusted him and possibly let him go — but he seems so mixed up with the Count in an "indexy" kind of way that I was afraid of taking the risk.

VAN HELSING: Friend John — we can only do as we think best: what else have we to hope for — except the pity of the good God!

> [*The folding doors open, admitting* HARKER, GODALMING *and* MISS MORRIS. *They have not removed their coats but take them off as they enter.*]

Well — my friends?

GODALMING: It's all right! An hour ago we found the last one of the six earth-boxes — and destroyed it.

VAN HELSING: Destroyed?

MORRIS: For him!

VAN HELSING: What exactly is your report?

HARKER: [*Referring to note book.*] He landed here with six of these packing cases — filled with his sacred earth. One remains in the Coach House at Carfax — the other five were distributed all over London, at each and every one of the houses I purchased for him. Fortunately, as the business had been done through me, I knew every address and had the right of entry. At ten o'clock yesterday morning we dealt with the first one — in the basement of 197 Jamaica Lane. Bermondsey — and between then and now we have located and sterilised the lot — with the sole exception of the one you told us to leave alone.

VAN HELSING: That is the one at Carfax. It is as well that we decided not to touch that one. Had we done so—the Count would have taken steps to frustrate our sterilizing the others—but now it is good, my friends—we know where for certain we shall find him tonight.

MORRIS: Say, Professor, he seems to have had no fancy for house property on the south side of London; his boxes were all scattered over the north and east.

VAN HELSING: That is easily understood, my friend—had they been on the south side, they would have been inaccessible to him being across running water! But tell me Harker—what precisely did you do with the boxes?

HARKER: We threw the lid off each, then spread the garlic evenly over the surface of the earth.

VAN HELSING: Then there remains only one he can possibly use— and that lies two hundred yards away from here. We shall make acquaintance with it tonight.

MORRIS: Say, Professor, did you see the evening paper carrying the "local interest" stuff? Reads queer to me.

VAN HELSING: I have not seen the paper. What is it about?

MORRIS: Godalming has it—let the Professor read it!

VAN HELSING: Well it certainly reads like the work of this unspeakable beast—I'll read it. [*Reads.*] "Westminster Gazette"—later afternoon edition. A Hampstead mystery. The neighbourhood of Hampstead is just at present exercised with a series of events which seem to run on lines parallel to those known to the writers of "headlines" as "The Kensington Horror" or "The Stabbing Woman" or "The Woman in Black". During the past two or three days, several cases have occurred of young children straying from home, or neglecting to return from their playing on the Heath. In all these cases the children were too young to give an intelligible account of themselves, but the consensus of their excuses is that they had been with a "Bu-ful Lady". It has always been late in the evening when they have been missed, and on two occasions they have not been found until early in the following morning; all the children have been slightly torn or wounded in the throat. The wounds seem such as might be made by a rat or a small dog—but they all tell the same story of being enticed away by a "Bu-ful Lady".

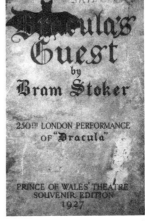

This special edition of Bram Stoker's story collection Dracula's Guest *was distributed to audience members as a souvenir of the play's 250th performance, at the Prince of Wales Theatre. Inside was another surprise—a flying cardboard bat, propelled by a rubber band, that shot out of the book when it was opened. (Courtesy of Jeanne Youngson)*

[*As* VAN HELSING *finishes reading he lowers paper and sits motionless looking straight in front of him—then slowly says:*]

My God—so soon!

GODALMING: What do you mean, Professor?

VAN HELSING: Oh! It is of no use to mince the matter any longer—Lord Godalming, you must prepare yourself for a great shock. You think that those small holes in the children's throats were made by the same that made the holes in Miss Lucy's?

GODALMING: I can only think so, Professor.

VAN HELSING: Then you are wrong. Would that it were so. But it is worse—far worse.

HARKER: In God's name, Professor—what do you mean?

VAN HELSING: [*Lowers himself into chair, covering his face with his hands.*] They were made by Miss Lucy herself! [*A pause—all remain staring hard at* VAN HELSING, *then* GODALMING *puts his hand to his head.* VAN HELSING *rises.*] Lord Godalming—you know we have work to do, this evening at sunset?

GODALMING: Yes—I am ready for that.

VAN HELSING: For what I think it right to do *afterwards*—I want permission now. It is, I know, much to ask—therefore may I ask that you promise me in the dark—so that afterwards you shall not blame yourself for anything?

MORRIS: That's frank, anyhow. I'll answer for the Professor. I don't quite see his drift—but I'll gamble he's dead right.

GODALMING: May I ask what it is we are to do?

VAN HELSING: I want you to come with me and to come in secret, to the churchyard at Hampstead.

GODALMING: Where poor Lucy is buried?

[VAN HELSING *bows.*]

And then where?

VAN HELSING: To enter the tomb.

GODALMING: And when in the tomb?

VAN HELSING: To open the coffin.

GODALMING: This is too much! This desecration of the grave of one who—

VAN HELSING: If I could spare you one pang, my poor friend—God knows I would—may I not go on? Miss Lucy is dead—is it not so? Then there can be no wrong in her. But if she not be dead—!

GODALMING: Good God, what do you mean? Has there been a mistake? Has she been buried alive?

VAN HELSING: I did not say she was alive. I did not think it, but I *do* say she is "un-dead".

Opposite: a page from Hamilton Deane's original script.

RENFIELD   The Fly - my dear sir - has one striking feature, its wings are typical of the aerial powers of the psychic faculties. The ancients did well - when they typified the soul as a butterfly !

SEWARD   Oh, it's a 'soul' you are after now - is it ?

RENFIELD   Oh no - oh no - I want no 'souls'. Life is all I want - and Blood is the life ! Life is a positive and perpetual entity, and by consuming a multitude of live things - no matter how low in the scale of creation, one may indefinitely prolong life - but I don't want any souls - indeed I don't - they would be no use to me - I couldn't eat them or - - -

SEWARD   But how are you to get the life, without getting the soul also ?

          RENFIELD looks puzzled.

A nice time you'll have some day when you are flying out there, with the souls of thousands of flies and spiders, and birds and cats, buzzing and twittering and miauing all round you. You've got their lives you know - and you must put up with their souls !

          RENFIELD puts his fingers in his ears,
          and shuts his eyes screwing them up
          tightly.

RENFIELD   To hell with you and your souls. Why do you plague me about souls ? Haven't I got enough to worry and distract me already without thinking of souls !

SEWARD   Renfield !

RENFIELD   Forgive me, Doctor, I forgot myself ! I am so worried in my mind that I am apt to be irritable. If you only knew the problem I have to face - you would pity and pardon me. Please don't put me in a "strait-jacket", I want to think, and I can't think freely when my body is confined !

SEWARD   Well, come now - wouldn't you like some sugar to spread out for your flies ?

RENFIELD   Flies ! (A look of animation comes over his face - then passes) Oh flies are but poor things !

GODALMING: Un-dead—not alive—what do you mean?

VAN HELSING: Lord Godalming, your permission to see to it that she becomes "true-dead".

GODALMING: You mean to—

VAN HELSING: Yes!

GODALMING: Are you mad? I shall not give my consent. I have a duty to do—in protecting her grave from outrage—and by God I shall do it.

VAN HELSING: My Lord Godalming! I too have a duty to do, a duty to others, a duty to you, a duty to the dead, and by God—I shall do it. All that I ask you *now* is that you listen! All that die—from the "preying" of the "un-dead" become themselves "un-dead" and prey on their kind. The career of this so unhappy young lady is but just begun. Those children whose blood she suck are not as yet much the worse, but if she remains an "un-dead," more and more they lose their blood, and by her power over them she compel them to come to her. But if she die—in truth—then all cease, the tiny wounds of the throats disappear, and they go back to their play—unknowing even of what has been. But—most blessed of all—when this now "un-dead" be made to rest as "true-dead"— then the soul of the poor Lucy whom you love—shall again be free—she shall take her place with the other angels.

GODALMING: And how do you propose to—?

VAN HELSING: There is but one way to make the "un-dead" a "true-dead"—to drive a stake through the heart.

GODALMING: Oh my God!

VAN HELSING: Be brave, my friend—and some day you shall thank me on your knees for insisting on this.

GODALMING: Van Helsing, sometimes I think we must all be mad and that we shall wake up to sanity in "strait-jackets." I don't know what to say or to think but I believe in you—you must do as you think fit.

VAN HELSING: Thank you, Lord Godalming—on behalf of all humanity—and now my friends I have more work for you to do— it would be good if you and Harker go direct now to the only earth-box left to the Count; the one which lies in the coach house at Carfax, and find out for me if he lies there now.

HARKER: Supposing he isn't there?

VAN HELSING: It will be something of grave importance to him that would keep him from his "day-slumber." But in any case in order to change he must return to his earth-box at sunset. Friend John,

Frederick Keen was one of several replacement Draculas during the play's long run in London.

have you found out the precise moment at which the sun sets today?

SEWARD: Yes! It sets at exactly six o'clock.

VAN HELSING: Good—at five minutes to six we shall leave here for Carfax.

HARKER: We'll go now—come along, Godalming.

[*Exeunt through folding doors.*]

VAN HELSING: Miss Morris, I am afraid that the work which lies ahead of us tonight is not suited to a woman—however much of pluck she has—so when we leave for Carfax you will remain with Madame Mina.

MORRIS: I just hate not to be in on this, Professor—but I understand. Say, at least you'll leave the weapons and other things to me.

VAN HELSING: [*Nods.*] They shall be ready. [MORRIS *and* HARKER *exit. After they have gone,* VAN HELSING *takes two or three strides across room, then faces* SEWARD.] There is one thing as yet I cannot understand; by what agency did those flowers I had tied myself round Madame's neck become detached? I am certain she would not remove them, nor would anything induce the Count to touch them, and yet when we found her, they were some feet away across the floor.

SEWARD: Perhaps the maid could throw some light on the subject. You remember we sent her to Mina.

VAN HELSING: [*Rings bell.*] You are right, my friend—we shall see her—you and I.

SEWARD: The girl is devoted to Mina, she's been in her service for a long time now—Mina swears by her!

[MAID *enters.*]

MAID: You rang, sir?

VAN HELSING: Yes—I would wish to speak to you a moment, about what happened that night when we left Madame in your care.

MAID: Why, I told you sir—I was in the room barely one minute when Madame sent me to fetch Mr. Harker.

[*She starts, looks apprehensively over her shoulder and twists her apron in her fingers.*]

VAN HELSING: [*Draws his breath—takes a quick look towards* SEWARD.] So-o-o! [*Walking quickly to the girl, he seizes thin ribbon round her neck, pulls it out, and discloses a crucifix.*] That crucifix—I placed

Actress Dora Jay prepares to give her all to the Dracula *cause.*

round Madame's neck that night. How comes it in your possession?

MAID: [*Bursts out crying.*] Oh, sir, I'm not a thief—indeed, indeed I'm not! Something impelled me to take away that crucifix and to remove the flowers from Madame's neck!

VAN HELSING: [*Quite gently.*] Something? What something—come now—tell me, I will not be hard on you. I know—perhaps more than you think.

MAID: I don't know, sir—but there seems to be some strange influence over me the last few days which makes me do things I had no intention of doing.

SEWARD: And can you not account for the "influence" at all?

MAID: Well, sir—the foreign gentleman was talking to me the other day—he said that I was a good "hypnotic" subject or something of the kind; and that I would be useful to him in his work—that he could compel me to do his bidding. I felt faint and drowsy—and everything seemed far away.

VAN HELSING: And then?

MAID: As he left the room I heard him say: "When my brain says 'Come' to you—you shall cross land or sea to do my bidding. When I 'will' you to do a thing it shall be done," and ever since then at odd moments I have had an impulse to do things which would never occur to me—in an ordinary way.

VAN HELSING: I see—and you put it down to his power of suggestion that you removed those flowers and that crucifix?

MAID: I can't account for it any other way, sir—but indeed I'm not a thief—I'm not! I'm not!

VAN HELSING: That will do—your punishment will surely come—but not through me. His power over you will cease shortly now. In the meantime resist any suggestions that he may make to you—and come straight to either Dr. Seward or myself. You may go.

MAID: Oh, thank you, sir—but you do believe that I am not a thief?

VAN HELSING: I believe you fully—you may go.

> [MAID *exits. The moment she has gone,* VAN HELSING *raises his hands above his head, as though appealing.*] Oh, God! God! What have we done—what has this poor thing done that we are so beset? Is it fate—or are all the powers of the Devil against us?
>
> [*He stops—then bursts out laughing, putting his hands over his face—he laughs and laughs.*

The master and the maid: Raymond Huntley subjugates his slave.

[*The folding doors open and* MINA *enters very slowly.* VAN HELSING *and* SEWARD *go to meet her. She is pale and worn looking—but not much more so than in Act I.*]

VAN HELSING: Oh, Madame Mina—you feel better?

MINA: Yes, thank you, Doctor. I have had a long sleep, and am much more myself now, but I couldn't remain up there alone—I couldn't—you don't mind my coming down Doctor—do you?

VAN HELSING: No—but at the first sign of fatigue, back you go. I am glad—so glad you are better—because I have not liked to ask you before what much I want to know.

MINA: About that night?

VAN HELSING: Yes! If it would not upset you to tell friend John and me.

MINA: There is not much to tell. When I sent the maid to fetch my husband, I tried to cross the room to close the curtains; the mist poured into the room, and outside I saw the face of a man—I knew him at once—the waxen complexion—the parted lips—the red eyes. For an instant my heart stood still. I screamed out and fell.

VAN HELSING: And then—

MINA: Then I heard your voices in the corridor, and he was gone in a flash—the rest you know. Oh, Professor, it's a dreadful thing to say, but I'm certain I am right—the man or thing that came to me out of the mist was—Count Dracula!

[*The two men rise abruptly and exchange a look.*]

VAN HELSING: I know, Madame!

MINA: You know?

VAN HELSING: I had hoped to keep the truth from you—but you have found it out for yourself. You have been the victim, as poor Miss Lucy was, of a Vampire; but thank God, in your case we are in time. And soon—very soon—you shall be freed from his evil influence, and all this you have been through shall seem like a dream.

MINA: Oh, God—if only I had the courage to kill myself.

VAN HELSING: [*Standing at back of her, with his hands on her shoulders.*] You must not die—least of all by your own hand. Until this "Thing" who has fouled your life is "true-dead" you must not die—for if he is still with the "Quick-un-dead" your death would make you forever as he is. On your living soul, I charge you that you do not even think of death till this great evil is past.

The following dialogue, based closely on Stoker's text, was censored from Mina's speech by the Lord Chamberlain: "I screamed out, and fell on the floor. I can remember his bending over me, and Oh, my God —pity me—he placed his reeking lips on my throat. I have a vague memory of something very sweet all round me and I seemed sinking into deep green water, and then everything went black. How long this horrible thing lasted I don't know—but it seemed ages before I came to, and saw him withdraw his awful, sneering mouth—and as I looked—it was dripping with fresh blood."

Actor Keith Pyott replaced
Raymond Huntley during the
1927 London run of Dracula.
(Courtesy of the Dracula
Society)

MINA: Oh! tell me, Professor, what *am* I to do?

VAN HELSING: My dear, you must leave everything to us. On consideration we think it is madness to call in the Police—as "proof" is non-existent, besides all Scotland Yard could not prevent the Count from changing his "form" at his "change time" and thereby slipping through their hands.

MINA: Then there is no hope of destroying this monster?

VAN HELSING: There is every hope, Madame Mina. The Count has various "lairs" or resting places in different parts of London— these we have "sterilized," leaving him only one he can use, and that one is at Carfax. Until the sun sets tonight he must retain whatever "form" he now has—and in order to "change" he must return to this earth-box because there is no other left to him. As the sun sets we shall be there and, if all goes well, he shall return from whence he came!

MINA: A woman feels so useless at such a time as this—but can't I help you in any way?

VAN HELSING: You can help us greatly, Madame Mina, by keeping your nerve, and believing that what we do, we do for the best— and for your sake, Madame.

[HARKER *and* GODALMING *enter through centre doors—the moment* HARKER *sees* MINA, *he goes straight to her.*]

HARKER: So you're down, dear—how are you now?

MINA: Better—ever so much better, for I have hope now—John, dear, the Professor has told me everything.

VAN HELSING: I thought it best that she should know!

HARKER: You know about—Dracula? [MINA *nods, and her fingers go to her throat.*] Are you afraid—dear?

MINA: I should be a baby to be afraid with all you men to guard and look after me—but John, dear, and all of you—I want you to bear something in mind. I know that you must destroy this "Vampire-thing" for his own sake as well as for the sake of us all. But it is not a work of hate. That poor soul, who has caused all this misery, is the saddest case of all. You must be pitiful to him too, though it may not keep you from destroying him.

HARKER: May God give him into my hands, long enough to destroy that earthly life of his, which we are aiming at. If beyond that I could send his soul for ever and ever to burning hell, I would do it!

MINA: Oh, hush dear, hush! Don't say such things. Just think, my dear, that perhaps some day I, too, may need such pity!

HARKER: Mina, to one thing I have made up my mind, dear—if through this monster of the other world you should become as he is, in the end you shall not go into that unknown and terrible world alone. Oh, but that's impossible now! We shall soon meet and I care for nothing except to wipe this brute off the face of Creation—I would sell my soul to do it.

VAN HELSING: Oh, no—no, my friend, God does not purchase souls in this wise, and the Devil, though he may purchase, does not keep Faith. But tell me, my friend, what news have you for me.

GODALMING: He was not at Carfax—so we went straight to his nearest place, which is in Maida Vale—in the Daimler. As we got to within fifty yards of it, he came down the steps, hailed a taxi, and drove in the direction of town. That was all we wanted to know, so we came straight back here.

VAN HELSING: He is evidently going the rounds of his "earth homes" to find some place of rest which we have not sterilized. He must return to Carfax. We shall not have long to wait now—I thought so.

GODALMING: Where is Miss Morris?

SEWARD: She is getting ready something which we may need tonight. [With a glance at MINA.]

GODALMING: Let's find her. Coming, old man?

HARKER: Right! I can stand anything but this suspense. [He crosses to MINA—touches her on the shoulder.]

MINA: [Leaning back and taking his hand.] God guard you tonight, dear!

> [HARKER smiles and pats her cheek—then, joining GODALMING—they both go out.]

VAN HELSING: Come, Madame—I will take you to your room—you are at least safe till sunset and after—well—we are all in God's hand!

> [MINA weakly smiles at SEWARD and goes out, leaning heavily on VAN HELSING's arm. As they go, the MAID enters from dining room, switches on lights, draws window curtains. SEWARD watches her intently. She goes out again through dining room door without speaking. SEWARD paces restlessly up and down for a few seconds, then picks up paper and starts to read. Suddenly, the folding doors are thrown open and REN- FIELD rushes in—in a state of abject terror—he comes downstage then rushes back and closes door.]

RENFIELD: For God's sake, doctor—save me! Save me from him—don't let him kill me!

SEWARD: Kill you—who? You must go back to your cell at once!

RENFIELD: No—not there—anywhere but there!

SEWARD: Explain yourself, man—what's the matter?

RENFIELD: [*Crouching on floor by* SEWARD.] That night when I implored you to let me go—and you refused—I couldn't speak outright then for I felt my tongue was tied. But I did my best to warn Mrs. Harker, didn't I?

SEWARD: Yes, yes—go on!

RENFIELD: Well, that night—he came to my cell window, in the mist, as I have seen him often before, but he was "solid" then, not a ghost, and his eyes were fierce; he beckoned me to the window and sneered at me, and his white face looked out of the mist with his red eyes gleaming. Then the dogs howled away beyond the dark trees, and he said I had betrayed him—and that with him the penalty for that was death!

SEWARD: How had you betrayed him?

RENFIELD: By warning Mrs. Harker. I don't care for her—I don't like pale people. I like them with lots of blood in them, and hers all seemed to have run out.

SEWARD: Why did you warn her, then?

RENFIELD: She has a gentle face—and there are few gentle faces in my life, and all of a sudden it made me mad to think that he was slowly but surely taking the life out of her.

SEWARD: Well, have you seen him since?

RENFIELD: Just now, a few minutes ago I saw the mist stealing in, and I knew my time had come so I grabbed it tight. I have heard that madmen have unnatural strength and I meant to use that power I had. He felt it, too, for he came out of the mist to struggle with me—I held tight—and I thought I was going to win, till I saw his eyes. They burned into me, and all my strength left me. He raised me up and flung me against the door, which an attendant, hearing the scuffle, was just opening. I jumped up and ran to you. You won't send me back where he can get me, will you, Doctor? I am mad, I know, and bad too, for I have taken thousands of lives—but they were only little lives. I am not like him—I would not take a human life—won't you send me away, Doctor—where he can't get me?

SEWARD: We'll see about that—meantime, remain here for a minute—you needn't be afraid; he dare not touch you in this

Playwright and actor-manager Hamilton Deane as he appeared in his later years. Following the disbanding of his theatre company, Deane appeared in several British films, including The Silver Darlings *(1947) and* The Case of Charles Peace *(1948). Deane can also be glimpsed as one of the courtiers in Laurence Olivier's production of* Hamlet *(1948). He died in 1958. (Courtesy of Ivan Butler)*

house. I must find Van Helsing. Sit down quietly till we return.

[*Left alone,* RENFIELD *crouches over the fire for a few minutes, then, standing upright, back to fire, he hums a tune, his fingers working convulsively. Suddenly he stops and "sniffs" the air — as a dog would — and a look of abject terror comes into his face. The folding doors open and* DRACULA *enters — they close and* DRACULA *comes straight down to centre stage with his eyes fixed on* RENFIELD.]

DRACULA: And so, you too, like the others, would play your brain against mine. You would help these men to hunt me, to frustrate me in my designs. You shall know *now* what it is to cross my path. And for the others — their turn shall come soon!

RENFIELD: Master! Master! I have never betrayed you. I never joined with anyone against you. I only told "her" to go away from here, but I did not say why —

DRACULA: Come here!

RENFIELD: [*Totters towards him and falls on his knees, clasping him.*] Master! For the love of God — let me live! I will do your bidding! I am your slave. I can't face the "Hereafter" with all those souls on my conscience — only let me live — let me live!

[*As he speaks he slowly raises his face towards* DRACULA's — *what he sees there makes him suddenly back away. He stands back to audience, facing* DRACULA, *his breath coming in gasps.* DRACULA *makes one step forward —* RENFIELD *squeals like a shot rabbit, then rushes up left past* DRACULA *and through window curtains.* DRACULA *follows — the curtains close behind them both — there is no sound, just a slight movement of the curtains, then* DRACULA *comes out alone, takes a step to his left and down stage — leaving full view of the curtains. As he does so,* VAN HELSING *and* SEWARD *enter. All the men "hold the picture" without movement for three seconds. Then,* DRACULA *speaks in a suave, assured manner.*]

DRACULA: So — some of you gentlemen have been paying "calls" at various houses of mine — I regret extremely I was not there to offer them my hospitality —

[*As he speaks a hand and arm fall through the curtains —* VAN HELSING *and* SEWARD *start.* DRACULA *does not move a muscle.* VAN HELSING *signals* SEWARD, *who quickly passes in front of* DRACULA, *draws curtains aside and discloses crumpled figure of* RENFIELD *with his head twisted back across window seat.*]

SEWARD: Good God! It's Renfield, poor, poor devil! Back broken!

[DRACULA *shrugs shoulders, turns leisurely to pass through door Right. Door opens—and* MISS MORRIS *stands in the way—a signal from* VAN HELSING *and she stolidly blocks* DRACULA's *exit.* DRACULA *turns left towards dining room—but* VAN HELSING *steps in front of it. He then quickly flings folding doors open and* HARKER *and* GODALMING *are outside. Without one word being spoken, they simultaneously close in on* DRACULA—*each one accelerating or retarding his advance, according to his distance from* DRACULA. *The latter backs slowly down stage till he stops himself at the back of sofa—then, finding himself cornered he lets go at them in a voice hysterical with mad rage, "snarling" his words out.*]

DRACULA: You think to baffle me — you — with your pale faces all in a row — like sheep in a butcher's; you shall be sorry yet, each one of you. You think you have left me without a place to rest — but I have more! Bah!

[*He raises his right arm—then lowers it quickly—there is a blinding white flash—they all recoil, then rush towards him. He has gone.*]

CURTAIN

A flash-box was used here to startle and distract audiences, blinding them momentarily while Dracula made his exit through a secret panel in the scenery. "Hamilton Deane was a gentle man," recalled Ivan Butler, "but his anger when these failed to go off (as inevitably happened at times) was awe-inspiring!"

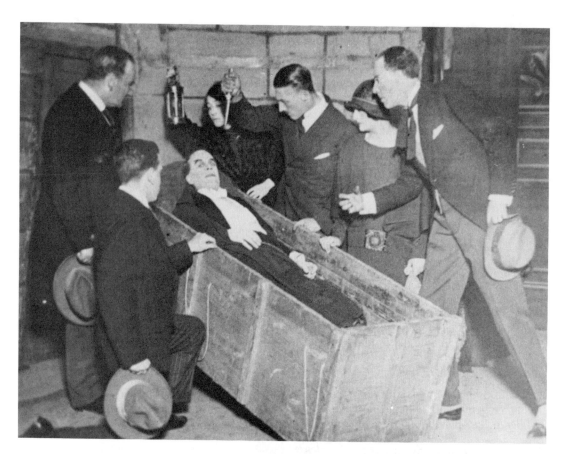

Edmund Blake, the first actor to portray Dracula in Hamilton Deane's adaptation, about to meet his end. Blake's real body was hidden under a realistic dummy with a shirt-front that spurt blood when stabbed—at least until the censors objected. Hamilton Deane, in the role of Van Helsing, is seen at right. (Courtesy of the Dracula Society)

Hamilton Deane used a dagger instead of a stake to dispatch Raymond Huntley at the conclusion of Dracula. In this photo, one of the trick coffin's folding panels is clearly visible. Their action obscured by a rising cloud of dust, the panels closed over the actor, creating the illusion of an empty box.

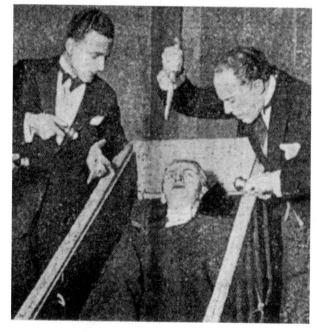

Epilogue

Takes place in the coach house at Carfax — a huge desolate barn of a place, thick with dust. Some old harness hangs on the walls which are fluffy and heavy with dust. An old Brougham, and an antiquated Dogcart are in the background. Dust is everywhere — and spiders' webs — and in the foreground centre stage there lies a huge wooden packing case or box, one end of which is tilted up. The stage cloth is painted dust colour with foot marks leading to centre from door which is down stage right. The cover is on the box. There is a half light just sufficient to let audience see the details. As the curtain rises there is absolute stillness for several seconds — then the jingling of keys is heard and the door opens slowly — daylight is seen outside. There enter, in the following order, VAN HELSING, HARKER, GODALMING *and* SEWARD; *the last one closes the door, and as he does so the first stroke of six is heard from a church clock outside. Each of the men carries an electric torch and the beams play round the coach house for a few seconds, then all of them are focussed on the earth box. No word is spoken, but* VAN HELSING *signals.*

The FOUR MEN *close round the box, completely covering* DRACULA *from the audience; there is a movement of* HARKER'S *arm — but the audience sees nothing of the killing. The door opens — and* MINA, *followed by* MISS MORRIS, *is seen in doorway holding a lantern. The men form a semi-circle round the body.* MINA *covers her face with her hands.*

MINA: Well — ?

HARKER: [*Goes to her, puts his arm right round her.*] Count Dracula is at rest.

VAN HELSING: "In Manas tuas Domine". [*He crosses himself.*]

THE CURTAIN FALLS

Here is Deane's original version of this scene, censored by the Lord Chamberlain: "[Dracula's] real body lies under the earth and to the right, the dummy body lies straight up and down the box. At the last strike of six — from the church clock — Van Helsing raises his hand and Harker first — then Morris and Godalming — plunge their knives into the heart — blood from the sponges at haft of knives, wells up on the white shirt front — the face gives a convulsive twist and shudder — Seward draws the cloak over the features — and the men stand up; the door opens — and Mina is seen in door-way holding a lantern — the men form a 'semicircle' round the body — Mina covers her face with her hands — dropping the lantern." Deane finally reached a compromise by having his stage manager Leslie Drayton devise a trick coffin along the lines of a magician's disappearing box, in which the vampire seemed to crumble bloodlessly into dust before the audience's eyes.

Bela Lugosi: Public Vampire Number One.
(Courtesy of Ronald V. Borst/Hollywood Movie Posters)

Hamilton Deane & John L. Balderston

Dracula

The Vampire Play

(1927)

Adapted from Bram Stoker's World-Famous Novel, "Dracula"

FULTON THEATRE

46th Street, Just West of Broadway

DILLER THEATRE CORPORATION, Lessee

A. L. Erlanger, President   C. B. Dillingham, Vice-President

Matinees Wednesday and Saturday

HORACE LIVERIGHT
Presents

"DRACULA"

The Vampire Play

Dramatized by
Hamilton Deane and John Balderston
From Bram Stoker's Famous Novel "Dracula"
Staged by IRA HARDS
Scenes by Joseph Physioc

CHARACTERS
(In Order of Their Appearance)

WELLS ....NEDDA HARRIGAN
JONATHAN HARKER...........................TERRENCE NEILL
DR. SEWARD..................................HERBERT BUNSTON
ABRAHAM vanHELSING.....................EDWARD VANSLOAN
R. M. RENFIELD................................BERNARD JUKES
BUTTERWORTH ....ALFRED FRITH
LUCY SEWARD...........................DOROTHY PETERSON
COUNT DRACULA.................................BELA LUGOSI

SYNOPSIS OF SCENES

ACT I.
Library in Dr. Seward's Sanatorium, at Purlev. Evening.

ACT II.
Lucy's Boudoir. Evening of the Following Day.

ACT III.
Scene 1—Same as Act I. Thirty-two hours later.
(Shortly before Sunrise.)

Scene 2—A Vault. Just after Sunrise.

Act One

The library on the ground floor of DR. SEWARD'S *Sanatorium at Purley. Room is medieval, the walls are stone with vaulted ceiling supported by two stone pillars, but is comfortably furnished in modern style. Wooden paneling around walls. Tapestries hang on the wall. Medieval fireplace in wall right. Fire burning. There is a divan right center, a large armchair right. At left, a desk with armchair back of it, a small chair to right of desk. Double doors in the rear wall. Large double window across angle of room, left rear, leading out into garden. The curtains are drawn. Door downstage left. Invisible sliding panel in bookcase rear wall right.*

MAID, *an attractive young girl, enters, showing in* JOHN HARKER. HARKER *is a young man of about twenty-five, handsome in appearance; a typical Englishman of the Public School class, but in manner direct, explosive, incisive and excitable.*

HARKER: [*Agitated.*] You're sure Miss Lucy is no worse?

MAID: [*Soothingly.*] Just the same, sir.

[DR. SEWARD *comes in, downstage left. He is an alienist of about fifty-five, intelligent, but a typical specialist who lives in a world of textbooks and patients, not a man of action or force of character. The* MAID *exits, closing doors.*]

SEWARD: Oh! John.

HARKER: [*As* SEWARD *extends hand.*] Doctor Seward. What is it? Why have you sent for me?

SEWARD: My dear John. I told you in my wire there was nothing new.

HARKER: You said "no change, don't worry," but to "come at once."

SEWARD: [*Approvingly.*] And you lost no time.

HARKER: I jumped in the car and burned up the road from London. Oh, Doctor, surely there must be something *more* we can do for Lucy. I'd give my life gladly if it would save her.

The American journalist and playwright John Lloyd Balderston, who re-wrote Hamilton Deane's Dracula for Broadway. His unproduced Broadway adaptation of Peggy Webling's Frankenstein (produced in England by Deane) became the basis for the classic 1931 film starring Boris Karloff. Balderston was intimately involved with many of the classic horror films of the 1930s, contributing to the screenplays of The Mummy (1932), Bride of Frankenstein (1935), and Mad Love (1935). Balderston's other screen work included the Academy Award-nominated The Lives of a Bengal Lancer (1935), The Prisoner of Zenda (1937) and Gaslight (1944), another Oscar nomination. He died in Beverly Hills in 1954.

SEWARD: I'm sure you would, my boy. You love her with the warm blood of youth, but don't forget I love my daughter, too. She's all I have. . . . You must see that nothing medical science can suggest has been left undone.

HARKER: [Bitterly.] Medical science couldn't do much for Mina. Poor Mina.

SEWARD: Yes, poor Mina. She died after these same incredible symptoms that my Lucy has developed.

HARKER: My Lucy too.

SEWARD: Our Lucy, then.

[Wild, maniacal laugh is heard offstage left.]

HARKER: Good God, what was that?

SEWARD: [Sits at desk.] Only Renfield. A patient of mine.

HARKER: But you never keep violent patients here in your sanatorium. Lucy mustn't be compelled to listen to raving madmen.

SEWARD: I quite agree, and I'm going to have him sent away. Until just lately he was always quiet. I'll be sorry to lose him.

HARKER: What!

SEWARD: An unusual case. Zoophagous.

HARKER: What's that?

SEWARD: A life-eating maniac.

HARKER: What?

SEWARD: Yes, he thinks that by absorbing lives he can prolong his own life.

HARKER: Good Lord!

SEWARD: Catches flies and eats them. And by way of change, he feeds flies to spiders. Fattens them up. Then he eats the spiders.

HARKER: Good God, how disgusting. [Sits.] But tell me about Lucy. [Leans over desk.] Why did you send for me?

SEWARD: Yesterday I wired to Holland for my old friend Van Helsing. He'll be here soon. The car has gone down to the station for him now. I'm going to turn Lucy's case over to him.

HARKER: Another specialist on anæmia?

SEWARD: No, my boy, whatever this may be, it's not anæmia, and this man, who speaks a dozen languages as well as his own, knows more about mysterious diseases than anyone alive.

HARKER: [Rises.] Heaven knows it's mysterious enough, but surely the symptoms are clear.

SEWARD: So were poor Mina's. Perfectly clear. [A dog howls at a distance. Other dogs take up the lugubrious chorus far and near. SEWARD

How The New York Critics Regard
DRACULA
New York's Newest Shudder!!!

"NOTHING MORE BLITHELY BLOOD - CURDLING SINCE 'THE BAT.' " —*Percy Hammond, Herald-Tribune.*

"SEE IT AND CREEP"—John Anderson, Post.

"WAS ENJOYED TO THE HILT—AUDIENCE QUAKED DELIGHTEDLY AT THE FULTON."
—*Alexander Woollcott, World.*

"Shivery as You Could Possibly Wish and Very Well Played."
—*Burns Mantle, News.*

"AN EVENING RICH IN HORROR."
—*Frank Vreeland, Telegram.*

"A Series of Spine-Creeping Thrills."
—*Walter Winchell, Graphic.*

"Brought Chills to Many Distinguished First Nighters." —*Robert Coleman, Mirror.*

"SHOULD BE SEEN BY ALL WHO LOVE THEIR MARROWS JOLTED, THEIR HAIR RAISED AND THEIR SLUMBERS TRAMPLED." —*Gilbert Gabriel, Sun.*

"DRACULA IS THE UNUSUAL IN PLAYS"
—*Arthur Pollock, Brooklyn Eagle.*

"IN A CLASS BY ITSELF! After Seeing About Every Thriller on Broadway in the Last 15 Years, This Is the First and Only One That Actually THRILLS for Three Acts."
—*Wall Street Journal.*

Actor Edward Van Sloan (1881–1964) first came to Horace Liveright's attention when he played the part of an Austrian psychiatrist in Hans Werfel's drama *Schweiger.* Immediately after the play closed, Liveright offered him another doctor part—Professor Van Helsing in *Dracula.* "I had been in five plays, none of which had lasted more than three weeks. I went into *Dracula,* figuring it would at least buy cakes and ale" for a fortnight, Van Sloan told the *San Francisco Chronicle* in 1932. "I proceeded to play it for twenty-two months, as *Dracula* romped merrily through colossal runs in New York, Philadelphia, Chicago, and out to the coast."

Edward Van Sloan

rises; crosses to fireplace.] There they are, at it again, every dog for a mile around.

HARKER: [*Crosses to window.*] They seem howls of terror.

SEWARD: We've heard that chorus every night since Mina fell ill.

HARKER: When I was traveling in Russia, and the dogs in the village barked like that, the natives always said wolves were prowling about.

SEWARD: [*Gets cigarette on mantel; lights it.*] I hardly think you'll find wolves prowling around Purley, twenty miles from London.

HARKER: Yet your old house might be in a wilderness. [*Looks out of window.*] Nothing in sight except that place Carfax that Count Dracula has taken.

SEWARD: [*Turning from fireplace.*] Your friend, the Count, came in again last evening.

HARKER: He's no friend of mine.

SEWARD: Don't say that. He knows that you and I gave our blood for Lucy as well as for Mina, and he's offered to undergo transfusion himself if we need another volunteer. [*Sits on divan.*]

HARKER: By Jove, that's sporting of him. I see I've misjudged him.

SEWARD: He seems genuinely interested in Lucy. If he were a young man I'd think . . .

HARKER: What!

SEWARD: But his whole attitude shows that it isn't that. We need sympathy in this house, John, and I'm grateful for it.

HARKER: So am I. Anyone who offers to help Lucy can have anything I've got.

SEWARD: Well, I think he does help Lucy. She always seems cheered up when he comes.

HARKER: That's fine. May I go to Lucy now?

SEWARD: [*Rises.*] We'll go together. [*Bell rings off.* HARKER *crosses to door left.* SEWARD *puts out cigarette in ashtray.*] That must be Van Helsing. You go ahead and I'll come presently.

[HARKER *exits.* MAID *shows in* ABRAHAM VAN HELSING, *who enters briskly. Man of medium height, in the early fifties, with clean-shaven, astute face, shaggy gray eyebrows and a mass of gray hair which is brushed backward showing a high forehead. Dark, piercing eyes set far apart; nervous, alert manner; an air of resolution, clearly a man of resourceful action. Incisive speech, always to the point; raps his words out sharply and quickly.* VAN HELSING *carries small black bag.*]

MAID: Professor Van Helsing.

SEWARD: [*He and* VAN HELSING *shake hands warmly as* MAID *goes out.*] My dear Van Helsing, I can never repay you for this.

VAN HELSING: Were it only a patient of yours instead of your daughter, I would have come. You once rendered me a service.

SEWARD: Don't speak of that. You'd have done it for me. [*Starts to ring.*] Let me give you something to eat ... [*Stopped by* VAN HELSING'*s gesture.*]

VAN HELSING: [*Places bag on table back of divan.*] I dined on the boat train. I do not waste time when there is work to do.

SEWARD: Ah, Van Helsing, you cast the old spell on me. I lean on you before you have been two minutes in my house.

VAN HELSING: You wrote of your daughter's symptoms. Tell me more of the other young lady, the one who died.

SEWARD: [*Shows* VAN HELSING *to chair right of desk.* SEWARD *sits at desk.*] Poor Mina Weston. She was a girl just Lucy's age. They were inseparable. She was on a visit here when she fell ill. As I wrote you, she just grew weaker, day by day she wasted away. But there were no anæmic symptoms, her blood was normal when analyzed.

VAN HELSING: You said you performed transfusion.

SEWARD: Yes, Sir William Briggs ordered that. [*Baring forearm.*] You see this mark? Well, Lucy herself, and her fiancee, John Harker, gave their blood as well.

VAN HELSING: So ... Three transfusions ... And the effect?

SEWARD: She rallied after each. The color returned to her cheeks, but the next morning she would be pale and weak again. She complained of *bad dreams*. Ten days ago we found her in a stupor from which nothing could rouse her. She ... died.

VAN HELSING: And ... the other symptoms?

SEWARD: None, except those two little marks on the throat that I wrote you about.

VAN HELSING: And which perhaps brought me here so quickly. What were they like?

SEWARD: Just two little white dots with red centers. [VAN HELSING *nods grimly.*] We decided she must have run a safety pin through the skin of her throat, trying in her delirium to fasten a scarf or shawl.

VAN HELSING: Perhaps. And your daughter's symptoms are the same?

SEWARD: Precisely. She too speaks of *bad dreams*. Van Helsing,

Horace Brisbin Liveright, the flamboyant publisher of the 1920s, was also an innovative theatrical producer who generated tremendous publicity (if not always box office receipts) for such plays as The Firebrand *(1924),* Hamlet in Modern Dress *(1925), and* An American Tragedy *(1926).* Dracula *proved to be his most lucrative theatrical endeavor, earning over $2 million on Broadway and on tour. Nonetheless, he foolishly signed away the movie rights, and lost his stage rights over nonpayment of royalties. One of the most colorful and influential figures of the Twenties, he was ruined in the stock market crash. Plagued by alcoholism, Liveright died almost penniless in 1933.*

you've lived in the tropics. May this not be something alien to our medical experience in England?

VAN HELSING: [*Grimly.*] It may indeed, my friend.

[*Laugh is heard from behind curtain at window.* VAN HELSING *rises, followed by* SEWARD *who crosses to window and draws curtains.* RENFIELD *is standing there. Repulsive youth, face distorted, shifty eyes, tousled hair.*]

SEWARD: [*Astounded, drawing* RENFIELD *into room.*] Renfield. How did you . . . ?

VAN HELSING: Who is this man?

SEWARD: [*Crosses to bell; rings.*] One of my patients. This is gross carelessness.

VAN HELSING: Did you hear us talking?

RENFIELD: Words . . . words . . . words . . .

SEWARD: Come, come, Renfield, you know you mustn't wander about this way. How did you get out of your room?

RENFIELD: [*Laughs.*] Wouldn't you like to know?

SEWARD: How are the flies? [*To* VAN HELSING.] Mr. Renfield makes a hobby of eating flies. I'm afraid you eat spiders, too, sometimes. Don't you, Renfield?

RENFIELD: Will you walk into my parlor, said the spider to the fly. Excuse me, Doctor, you have not introduced me to your friend.

SEWARD: [*Reprovingly.*] Come, come, Renfield.

VAN HELSING: Humor him.

[*Enter* MAID.]

SEWARD: Tell the Attendant to come here at once.

MAID: Yes, sir. [*Exits.*]

SEWARD: Oh, very well. Professor Van Helsing, Mr. Renfield, a patient of mine.

[VAN HELSING *steps toward him. They shake hands.* VAN HELSING *rubs* RENFIELD's *fingers with his thumb and* RENFIELD *jerks hand away.*]

RENFIELD: Ah, who does not know of Van Helsing! Your work, sir, in investigating certain obscure diseases, not altogether unconnected with forces and powers that the ignorant herd do not believe exist, has won you a position that posterity will recognize.

[*Enter* ATTENDANT *dressed in uniform. He starts at seeing*

Brooks Atkinson reviewed *Dracula* for *The New York Times*: "Dramatizing Bram Stoker's famous novel of a quarter-century ago, and playing it in the theatre, the various entrepreneurs have done extraordinarily well with their initial act, and rather less with the two remaining. When they are treating of this weird force as a mystery they send the customary shudders of apprehension down the back, and *Dracula* holds its audience nervously expectant. When in the next two acts the atmosphere becomes more realistic than occult, the effect is not so horribly fascinating. Played more swiftly, fiercely and mysteriously, *Dracula* could doubtless scare the skeptics out of several year's growth and into complete submission."

RENFIELD, *then looks at* SEWARD *sheepishly.*]

SEWARD: [*As severely as his mild nature permits.*] Butterworth, you have let your patient leave his room again.

ATTENDANT: Blimme, sir, I locked the door on 'im, and I've got the key in my pocket now.

SEWARD: But this is the second time. Only last night you let him escape and he tried to break into Count Dracula's house across the grounds.

ATTENDANT: 'E didn't get out the door this time, sir, and it's a drop of thirty feet out of the windows. [*Crosses to* RENFIELD.] He's just a bloomin' eel. Now you come with me. [*As they start toward door; holds* RENFIELD *by coat collar and right arm.*]

SEWARD: Renfield, if this happens again you will get no more sugar to spread out for your flies.

Both Raymond Huntley and Bernard Jukes crossed the Atlantic to reprise their Dracula *roles for American audiences.*

Opposite: Advertising art for the Horace Liveright production.

RENFIELD: [*Drawing himself up.*] What do I care for flies . . . *now?* [ATTENDANT *gives* VAN HELSING *a look.*] Flies. Flies are but poor things. [*As he speaks he follows with his eyes a fly.* ATTENDANT *sees fly too; releases* RENFIELD *indulgently. With a sweep of his hand he catches fly, holds closed hand to ear as if listening to buzz of fly as he crosses a few steps, then carries it to his mouth. Then seeing them watching him, releases it quickly.*] A low form of life. Beneath my notice. I don't care a pin about flies.

ATTENDANT: Oh, doncher? Any more o' yer tricks and I'll take yer new spider away.

RENFIELD: [*Babbles; on knees.*] Oh, no, no! Please, dear Mr. Butterworth, please leave me my spider. He's getting so nice and fat. When he's had another dozen flies he'll be just right, just right. [*Gives little laugh. Rubs hands together, then catches fly and makes gesture of eating.*]

VAN HELSING: Come, Mr. Renfield, what makes you want to eat flies?

RENFIELD: [*Rises.*] The wings of a fly, my dear sir, typify the aerial powers of the psychic faculties.

SEWARD: [*To* ATTENDANT, *wearily.*] Butterworth, take him away.

VAN HELSING: One moment, my friend. [*To* RENFIELD.] And the spiders?

RENFIELD: [*Impressively.*] Professor Van Helsing, can you tell me why that one great spider lived for centuries in the tower of the old Spanish church — and grew and grew? He never ate, but he drank, and he *drank.* He would come down and drink the oil of all the church lamps.

SEWARD: [*To* ATTENDANT.] Butterworth.

RENFIELD: One moment, Doctor Seward . . . [VAN HELSING *gets wolfsbane from bag on table.*] I want you to send me away, now, *tonight,* in a straight waistcoat. Chain me so I can't escape. This is a sanatorium, not a lunatic asylum. This is no place for me. My cries will disturb Miss Lucy, who is ill. They will give your daughter *bad dreams,* Doctor Seward, *bad dreams.*

SEWARD: [*Soothingly.*] We'll see about all this in the morning. [*Nods to* ATTENDANT, *who moves toward* RENFIELD.]

VAN HELSING: Why are you so anxious to go?

RENFIELD: [*Crosses to* VAN HELSING; *hesitates, then with gesture of decision.*] I'll tell *you.* Not that fool Seward. He wouldn't understand. But you . . . [*A large bat dashes against window.* RENFIELD *turns to the window, holds out his hands and gibbers.*] No, no, no, I wasn't going to say anything . . .

HORACE LIVERIGHT *presents*

DRACULA
THE WORLD FAMOUS VAMPIRE THRILLER

DRAMATIZED by HAMILTON DEAN and JOHN L. BALDERSTON

from BRAM STOKER'S FAMOUS NOVEL DRACULA

STAGED BY IRA HARDS   . . .   SCENES BY JOSEPH PHYSIOC

[ATTENDANT *crosses up; watches* RENFIELD.]

SEWARD: What was that?

RENFIELD: [*Looks out window, then turns.*] It was a bat, gentleman. Only a bat! Do you know that in some islands of the Eastern seas there are bats which hang on trees all night? And when the heat is stifling and sailors sleep on the deck in those harbors, in the morning *they* are found dead men . . . white, even as Miss Mina was.

SEWARD: What do you know of Miss Mina? [*Pause.*] Take him to his room!

VAN HELSING: [*To* SEWARD.] Please! [*To* RENFIELD.] Why are you so anxious to be moved from here?

RENFIELD: To save my soul.

VAN HELSING: Yes?

RENFIELD: Oh, you'll get nothing more out of me than that. And I'm not sure I hadn't rather stay . . . After all, what is my soul good for? Is not . . . [*Turns to window.*] . . . *what I am to receive worth* the loss of my soul?

"Madmen have great strength."
Renfield (Bernard Jukes) vividly
demonstrates his point.

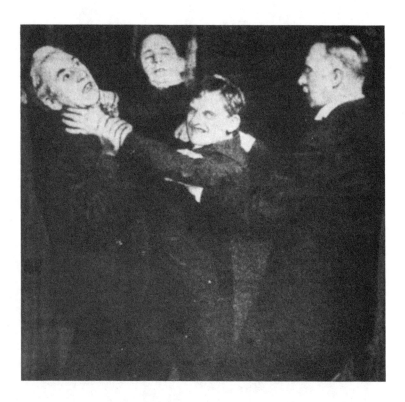

SEWARD: [*Lightly.*] What's got him thinking about souls? Have you the souls of those flies and spiders on your conscience?

RENFIELD: [*Puts fingers in his ears, shuts eyes, distorts face.*] I forbid you to plague me about souls! I don't want their *souls*. All I want is their life. The blood is the life . . .

VAN HELSING: So?

RENFIELD: That's in the Bible. What use are souls to me? [*To* VAN HELSING.] I couldn't eat them or dr . . . [*Breaks off suddenly.*]

VAN HELSING: Or drink . . . [*Holding wolfsbane under his nose,* RENFIELD's *face becomes convulsed with rage and loathing. He leaps back.*]

RENFIELD: You know too much to live, Van Helsing! [*He suddenly lunges at* VAN HELSING. SEWARD *and* ATTENDANT *shout at the attack and as they drag* RENFIELD *to door he stops struggling and says clearly:*]

RENFIELD: I'll go quietly. [SEWARD *lets go of him.*] I warned you to send me away. Doctor Seward, if you don't you must answer for my soul before the judgment seat of God!

> [RENFIELD *and* ATTENDANT *exit. Wild laughter can be heard off.* VAN HELSING *puts wolfsbane in bag as* SEWARD *closes door.*]

SEWARD: My friend, you're not hurt?

VAN HELSING: No.

SEWARD: My deepest apologies. You'll think my place shockingly managed . . .

> [VAN HELSING *waves apology aside with impatient gesture.*]

What was your herb that excited him so?

VAN HELSING: Wolfsbane. [*A little look out of window as he crosses.*]

SEWARD: Wolfsbane? What's that? I thought I knew all the drugs in the pharmacopoeia.

VAN HELSING: One of the . . . eremophytes. Pliny the Elder mentions the plant. It grows only in the wilds of Central Russia.

SEWARD: But why did you bring it with you?

VAN HELSING: It is a form of preventive medicine.

SEWARD: Well, we live and learn. I never heard of it.

VAN HELSING: Seward, I want you to have that lunatic securely watched.

SEWARD: Anything you say, Professor Van Helsing, but it's my Lucy I want you to look after first.

VAN HELSING: I want to keep this man under observation.

SEWARD: [*Annoyed and hurt.*] An interesting maniac, no doubt, but

In the opinion of *The New York Sun*, "*Dracula* is dedicated to that public which asks no more of drama than to be knocked out cold and be sent home on a shudder." The *Sun* called the play "a luxurious delirium, a literary Walpurgis, a spaciously harrowing legend, brimful and incarnadined with the eerie gymnastics of the grewsome." The reviewer, Gilbert Gabriel, admitted that "I found much of *Dracula* terribly entertaining. Sometimes the chaste Ibsen side of me said pish tush, tommyrot and unavailing things like that. Sometimes I had to grunt like a grown-up over such foolish sights as a bat which joggled around on the backdrop with all the liveliness of yesterday's washrag. But I was bullied out of noting lacunae like that, not by the gossip, for instance, that in London the bat was a still more dejected object on the end of a six-inch hawser, but by the sheer animal horror of the story. It doesn't do to stick out your tongue at a werewolf."

surely you'll see my daughter.

VAN HELSING: I must see the records of his case.

SEWARD: But Doctor . . .

VAN HELSING: Do you think I have forgotten why I am here?

SEWARD: [*As they start to go out left.*] Forgive me. Of course I'll show you the records, but I don't understand why you're so curious about Renfield, because in your vast experience . . .

[*They exit. The room is empty for a few seconds; then* LUCY *enters, supported by* HARKER. *She is a beautiful girl of twenty, clad in filmy white dressing gown, her face unnaturally pale. She walks with difficulty. Round her throat is wound a scarf. She crosses to desk and leans on it as* HARKER *closes door.*]

HARKER: Why, I thought they were here, Lucy.

LUCY: John, do you think this new man will be any better than the others?

HARKER: [*Moving her to divan.*] I'm sure he will. Anyway, Lucy, now that I'm back I'm going to stay with you till you get over this thing.

LUCY: [*Delighted.*] Oh, John. But can you? Your work in town?

HARKER: [*Seating her, then sitting next to her.*] You come first.

LUCY: [*A change comes over her.*] I . . . don't think you'd better stay, John. [*A look about room.*] Sometimes . . . I feel that I want to be alone.

HARKER: My dear. How can you say that you don't want me with you when you're so ill? You love me, don't you? [*Taking her hand.*]

LUCY: [*Affectionately.*] Yes, John, with all my soul.

HARKER: Just as soon as you're well enough I'm going to take you away. We'll be married next month. We won't wait till June. We'll stretch that honeymoon month to three months and the house will be ready in July.

LUCY: [*Overjoyed.*] John, you think we could?

HARKER: Of course, why not? My mother wanted us to wait, but she'll understand, and I want to get you *away* . . . [*Starts to kiss her. She shudders as he does so.*] Why do you shrink when I kiss you? You're so cold, Lucy, always so cold . . . now . . .

LUCY: [*With tenderness but no hint of passion.*] Forgive me, dear. I am yours, all yours. [*Clings to him. He embraces her. She sinks back.*] Oh, John, I'm so tired . . . so tired.

[SEWARD *and* VAN HELSING *return.*]

SEWARD: Lucy dear, this is my old friend, Professor Van Helsing.

In its appraisal of *Dracula*, *Time* recalled the initial impact of Stoker's novel: "So horrible were its beastly visions that many a maid fell helpless with hysterics; mothers banned the book, after reading it secretly themselves, and fainting." The magazine noted, however, that attitudes had changed considerably in the thirty intervening years. "Now maidens can see grisly horror, and withdraw between acts to smoke a cigarette and talk calmly of their minor vices. But when they are in the theatre they can scarcely resist *Dracula*; nor can their stalwart escorts. It is a chamber of horrors to raise the most jaded hair. Viewed technically it has its faults of mechanics and an occasional unevenness of interest. It is well, but not perfectly played. Yet the material is morbidly magnificent. And of course it is all perfectly silly."

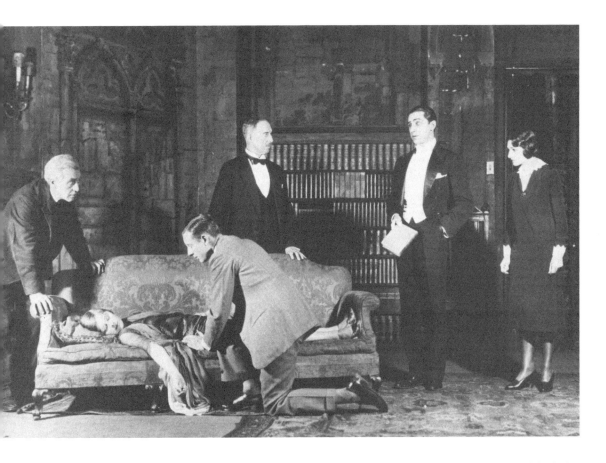

[*She sits up; extends her hand to him.*]

VAN HELSING: My dear Miss Seward . . . [*He kisses* LUCY's *hand.*] . . .
you don't remember poor old Van Helsing. I knew you when you
were a little girl. So high . . . and now what charm, what beauty. A
little pale, yes, but we will bring the roses back to the cheeks.

LUCY: You were so kind to come, Professor.

VAN HELSING: And this, no doubt, is the fortunate young man you
are to marry?

SEWARD: Yes, John Harker, Professor.

HARKER: Look here, Professor. I'm not going to get in your way, but
if Doctor Seward will have me I'm going to make him give me a
bed here until Lucy gets over this thing. [*Turns to* SEWARD.] It's
absolute hell, being away in London, and of course I can't do any
work.

SEWARD: You're most welcome to stay, my boy.

*Feigning ignorance of the fright
he has just caused, Dracula
plays the part of the concerned
neighbor. Left to right: Edward
Van Sloan, Dorothy Peterson,
Terrence Neill, Herbert
Bunston, Bela Lugosi and
Nedda Harrigan. (Courtesy of
Ronald V. Borst/Hollywood
Movie Posters)*

Dramatic antecedent: At right, T.P. Cooke, in The Vampire *(1820) wore not only a cloak, but a kilt. Above: Bela Lugosi and Dorothy Peterson created a similar tableau in the 1920s.*

VAN HELSING: Indeed, yes. I should have asked you to stay. I may need you. [*Takes chair from desk to left of divan; turns to* LUCY.] Now lie back, so . . . [*Examines her eyelids carefully and feels her pulse.*] And now tell me when did this, this weakness first come upon you? [*Sits, after examining eyelids; looks at her gums, examines tips of fingernails, then takes out watch as he feels her pulse.*]

LUCY: Two nights after poor Mina was buried I had . . . a bad dream.

VAN HELSING: [*Releases pulse, after looking at watch.*] A bad dream? Tell me about it.

LUCY: I remember hearing dogs barking before I went to sleep. The air seemed oppressive. I left the reading lamp lit by my bed, but when the dream came there seemed to come a mist in the room.

VAN HELSING: Was the window open?

LUCY: Yes, I always sleep with my window open.

VAN HELSING: Oh, of course, you're English. [*Laughs.*] We Continentals are not so particular about fresh air. And then . . .

LUCY: The mist seemed so thick I could just see the lamp by my bed, a tiny spark in the fog, and then . . . [*Hysterically.*] I saw two red eyes staring at me and a livid white face looking down on me out of the mist. It was horrible, horrible!

[HARKER *makes move toward her.* VAN HELSING *stops him by a gesture.*]

VAN HELSING: There, there . . . [*Soothingly, taking her hands from her face.*] Go on, please.

LUCY: [*Gives little start when* VAN HELSING *touches her hands. Looks at* HARKER *and starts; and at* SEWARD *and starts, then at* VAN HELSING *and relaxes.*] The next morning my maid could scarcely wake me. I felt weak and languid. Some part of my life seemed to have gone from me.

VAN HELSING: There have been other such dreams?

LUCY: Nearly every night since then has come the mist . . . the red eyes and that awful face.

[*She puts hands to her face again.* VAN HELSING *soothes her; ad libs, as he takes her hands from face, "There, there, now."*]

SEWARD: We've tried transfusion twice. Each time she recovered her strength.

LUCY: But then would come another dream. And now I dread the night. I know it seems absurd, Professor, but please don't laugh at me.

"*Dracula* is fun," opined *Vogue.* "It would probably be more fun were it less shoddily produced and performed. The tempo is terrible. But for Bernard Jukes's, the acting is desultory. Bela Lugosi as the Vampire resembles uncannily Walter Hampden in his more consciously impressive moments—the profile moments." *Vogue* complained that the "stage effects are crude and musty and appear to take a perverse delight in functioning wrong. Or, perhaps they and the stagehands who manipulate them share with the audience the shiveriness of the play. On second thought, the shoddiness of the production and performances may add to the merriment, may, indeed, create it. If the piece were better done, it might not be so amusing."

VAN HELSING: I'm not likely to laugh. . . .

> [*Gently, without answering, he unwinds scarf from her throat. She puts hand up to stop him and cries, "No, no." A look at* HARKER *when her neck is bare. As* VAN HELSING *does so he starts, then quickly opens small black bag on table and returns with microscope; examines two small marks on throat.* LUCY *with eyes closed. Controlling himself with difficulty,* VAN HELSING *puts microscope back in bag, closes it, puts back chair by desk.*]

And how long have you had these little marks on your throat?

> [SEWARD *and* HARKER *start violently and come to divan. They look at each other in horror.*]

LUCY: Since . . . that first morning.

HARKER: Lucy, why didn't you tell us?

SEWARD: Lucy, you've worn that scarf around your throat . . . to hide them!

> [LUCY *makes convulsive clutch at throat.*]

VAN HELSING: Do not press her. Do not excite her. [*To* LUCY.] Well?

LUCY: [*Constrained; to* SEWARD *and* HARKER.] I was afraid they'd worry you, for I knew that . . . Mina had them.

VAN HELSING: [*With assumed cheerfulness.*] Quite right, Miss Lucy, quite right. They're nothing, and old Van Helsing will see that these . . . dreams trouble you no more.

MAID: [*Appears at door.*] Count Dracula.

> [DRACULA *enters. He is a tall, mysterious man of about fifty. Polished and distinguished. Continental in appearance and manner.* LUCY *registers attraction to* DRACULA.]

SEWARD: Ah, good evening, Count.

DRACULA: Gentlemen . . . [*He bows to men; then goes to the divan and bows in courtly fashion.*] Miss Seward, how are you? You are looking more yourself this evening.

> [LUCY *registers thrill. Alternate moods of attraction and repulsion, unaccountable to herself, affect* LUCY *in* DRACULA'*s presence. But this should be suggested subtly.*]

LUCY: [*Quite natural.*] I feel better already, Count, now that father's old friend has come to help me.

Opposite: The backbend swoon, the kiss, the bite . . . Raymond Huntley enacted this moment thousands of times on stage between 1926 and 1930. Although Bela Lugosi would gain world fame from the role, it was Raymond Huntley who familiarized most audiences with the character. (The Harvard Theatre Collection)

[DRACULA *turns to* VAN HELSING. LUCY *looks up at* DRAC-ULA, *recoils, and turns to* HARKER.]

SEWARD: Count Dracula, Professor Van Helsing.

[*The two men bow.*]

DRACULA: A most distinguished scientist, whose name we know even in the wilds of Transylvania. [*To* SEWARD.] But I interrupt a consultation.

SEWARD: Not at all, Count. It's good of you to come, and we appreciate your motives.

HARKER: Doctor Seward has just told me of your offer, and I can't thank you enough.

DRACULA: It is nothing. I should be grateful to be permitted to help Miss Lucy in any way.

LUCY: But you do, Count. I look forward to your visits. They seem to make me better.

VAN HELSING: And so I arrive to find a rival in the field.

DRACULA: [*Crosses to* LUCY.] You encourage me, Miss Seward, to make them more frequent, as I should like to.

LUCY: [*Looking at him fixedly.*] I am always glad to see you.

DRACULA: Ah, but you have been lonely here. And my efforts to amuse you with our old tales will no longer have the same success, now that you have Professor Van Helsing with you, and especially now that Mr. Harker is to remain here.

HARKER: How did you know I was going to stay, Count?

DRACULA: [*Little start.*] Can the gallant lover ask such a question? I inferred it, my friend.

HARKER: You're right. Nothing is going to shift me now until Lucy's as fit as a fiddle again.

DRACULA: Nothing?

LUCY: Please come as before, Count, won't you?

[DRACULA *bows to her; kisses her hand.* VAN HELSING *meanwhile has been talking to* MAID.]

VAN HELSING: . . . you understand, you will not answer bells. She must not be alone for a single moment under any circumstances, you understand.

[*As* DRACULA *crosses to below desk,* LUCY *leans toward him, extends her hand, then recovers herself.* VAN HELSING *registers that he sees her look at* DRACULA.]

Opposite: A Washington D.C. cartoonist provided newspaper readers with this memorable portrait of Raymond Huntley when Dracula *opened in the nation's capitol in 1928.*

MAID: Yes, sir.

VAN HELSING: [*To* LUCY.] Good. Your maid will take you to your room. Try to rest for a little, while I talk to your father.

[MAID *comes to divan to get* LUCY. *Pause, as* LUCY *looks at* DRACULA.]

SEWARD: Wells, remember, don't leave her alone for a moment.

MAID: Oh, no, sir.

[LUCY *exchanges a long look with* DRACULA *as* MAID *takes her out.*]

The accent and inflections we now immediately associate with the character of Dracula was partially the result of Bela Lugosi's difficulties with English. (John Balderston recalled that the Hungarian actor had to be directed, as a compromise, in French.) Lugosi, whose failure to master English thoroughly caused lifelong career problems, learned his lines for *Dracula* phonetically—a gambit that worked only so long as the other performers didn't flub a cue.

DRACULA: Professor Van Helsing, so you have come from the land of the tulip, to cure the nervous prostration of this charming girl. I wish you all the success.

VAN HELSING: Thank you, Count.

DRACULA: Do I appear officious, Doctor Seward? I am a lonely man. You are my only neighbors when I am here at Carfax, and your trouble has touched me greatly.

SEWARD: Count, I am more grateful for your sympathy than I can say.

VAN HELSING: You, like myself, are a stranger in England, Count?

DRACULA: Yes, but I love England and the great London ... so different from my own Transylvania, where there are so few people and so little opportunity.

VAN HELSING: Opportunity, Count?

DRACULA: For my investigations, Professor.

SEWARD: I hope you haven't regretted buying that old ruin across there?

DRACULA: Oh, Carfax is not a ruin. The dust was somewhat deep, but we are used to dust in Transylvania.

HARKER: You plan to remain in England, Count?

DRACULA: I think so, my friend. The walls of my castle are broken, and the shadows are many, and I am the last of my race.

HARKER: It's a lonely spot you've chosen ... Carfax.

DRACULA: It is, and when I hear the dogs howling far and near I think myself back in my Castle Dracula with its broken battlements.

HARKER: Ah, the dogs howl there when there are wolves around, don't they?

DRACULA: They do, my friend. And they howl here as well, although there are no wolves. But you wish to consult the anxious father and the great specialist. . . . May I read a book in the study? I am so anxious to hear what the Professor says . . . and to learn if I can be

Till death do us part: Bela Lugosi interrupts the wedding plans of Hazel Whitmore and Don Woods.

of any help.

SEWARD: By all means, Count. [DRACULA *bows; exits.* SEWARD *watches him leave. Dogs howl offstage.*] Very kind of Dracula, with his damned untimely friendliness, but now what about my daughter?

HARKER: Yes, Professor, what do you think is the matter with Lucy?

VAN HELSING: [*Crosses to window, looks out. Long pause before he speaks.*] Your patient, that interesting Renfield, does not like the smell of wolfsbane.

SEWARD: Good Heavens. What has that got to do with Lucy?

VAN HELSING: Perhaps nothing.

HARKER: In God's name, Professor, is there anything unnatural or occult about this business?

SEWARD: Occult? Van Helsing! Oh . . .

VAN HELSING: Ah, Seward, let me remind you that the superstitions of today are the scientific facts of tomorrow. Science can now transmute the electron, the basis of all matter, into energy, and what is that but the dematerialization of matter? Yet dematerialization has been known and practiced in India for centuries. In Java I myself have seen things.

SEWARD: My dear old friend, you can't have filled up your fine old brain with Eastern moonshine.

VAN HELSING: Moonshine?

SEWARD: But anyway, come now, what about my daughter?

VAN HELSING: Ah! Seward, if you won't listen to what will be harder to believe than any Eastern moonshine, if you won't forget your textbooks . . . keep an open mind, then, Seward. Your daughter's life may pay for your pig-headedness.

HARKER: Go on, go on, Professor!

SEWARD: I am listening.

VAN HELSING: Then I must ask you to listen calmly to what I am going to say. Sit down. [VAN HELSING *crosses to window; closes curtains.* SEWARD *and* HARKER *exchange glances, then both look at* VAN HELSING *as they sit.*] You have both heard the legends of Central Europe, about the Werewolf, the Vampires?

SEWARD: You mean ghosts, who suck the blood of the living?

VAN HELSING: If you wish to call them ghosts. I call them the undead.

HARKER: [*Quickly.*] For God's sake, man, are you suggesting that Mina, and now Lucy . . .

SEWARD: [*Interrupting.*] Of course, I have read these horrible folk tales of the Middle Ages, Van Helsing, but I know you better than to suppose . . .

VAN HELSING: [*Interrupting.*] That I believe them? I *do* believe them.

SEWARD: [*Incredulously.*] You mean to tell us that vampires actually exist and . . . and that Mina and Lucy have been attacked by one?

VAN HELSING: Your English doctors would all laugh at such a theory. Your police, your public would laugh. [*Impressively.*] *The strength of the vampire is that people will not believe in him.*

SEWARD: [*Shaking head.*] Is this the help you bring us?

VAN HELSING: [*Much moved.*] Do not despise it.

HARKER: [*To* SEWARD.] Doctor, this case has stumped all your specialists. [*To* VAN HELSING.] Go on, Professor.

VAN HELSING: Vampires are rare. Nature abhors them, the forces of

good combine to destroy them, but a few of these creatures have lived on for centuries.

HARKER: [*Excited.*] What *is* a vampire?

VAN HELSING: A vampire, my friend, is a man or a woman who is dead and yet not dead. A thing that lives after its death by drinking the blood of the living. It must have blood or it dies. Its power lasts only from sunset to sunrise. During the hours of the day it must rest in the earth in which it was buried. But, during the night, it has the power to prey upon the living. [*Incredulous move from* SEWARD.] My friend, you are thinking you will have to put me amongst your patients?

SEWARD: Van Helsing, I don't know what to think but I confess I simply can't follow you.

HARKER: What makes you think that Lucy has been attacked by such a creature?

VAN HELSING: [*From now on dominating them.*] Doctor Seward's written account of these ladies' symptoms at once aroused my suspicion. Anæmia? The blood of three men was forced into the veins of Miss Mina. Yet she died from loss of blood. Where did it go? Had your specialist any answer? The vampire attacks the throat. He leaves two little wounds, white with red centers. [HARKER *rises slowly.*] Seward, you wrote me of those two marks on Miss Mina's throat. An accident with a safety pin, you said. So I thought, I suspected, I did not know, but I came on the instant, and what do I find? These same wounds on Miss Lucy's throat. Another safety pin, Doctor Seward?

SEWARD: Do you mean to say that you've built up all this nightmare out of a safety pin? It's true I can't make out why she hid those marks from us.

VAN HELSING: I could tell you that.

SEWARD: [*Pause.*] What! I don't believe it. Of course Lucy's trouble can't be *that.*

HARKER: I do believe it. This theory accounts for all the facts that nobody has been able to explain. We'll take her away where this thing can't get at her.

VAN HELSING: She will not want to go.

SEWARD: What!

VAN HELSING: If you force her, the shock may be fatal.

HARKER: But why won't she go if we tell her that her life depends on it?

VAN HELSING: Because the victim of the vampire becomes his

The London Draculas wore pale white makeup, but Horace Liveright liked his vampires green. When Raymond Huntley took over Lugosi's role and balked at the reptilian effect, Liveright angrily threatened to file a grievance action with Actors Equity. Huntley relented and showed up for the next performance in leprechaun tints. "I thought it was just bloody nonsense," Huntley recalled in 1989.

creature, linked to him in life and after death.

SEWARD: [*Incredulous, shocked; rises.*] Professor, this is too much!

HARKER: Lucy become an unclean thing, a demon?

VAN HELSING: Yes, Harker. *Now* will you help me?

HARKER: Yes, anything. Tell me what to do.

VAN HELSING: It is dangerous work. Our lives are at stake, but so is Miss Lucy's life, so is her soul. We must stamp out this monster.

HARKER: How can we stamp it out now?

VAN HELSING: This undead thing lies helpless by day in the earth or tomb in which it was buried.

SEWARD: A corpse, in a coffin?

VAN HELSING: A corpse, if you like, but a living corpse, sustained by the blood of the living. If we can find its earth home, a stake driven

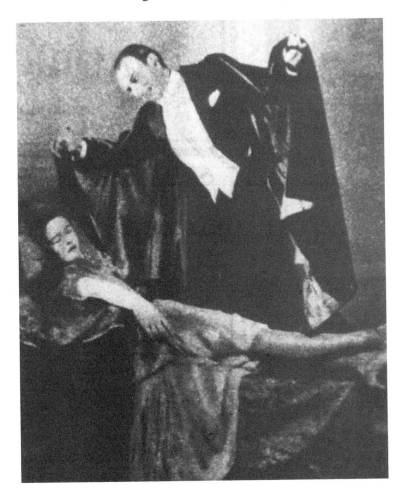

Raymond Huntley and Joan Colburn.

through the heart destroys the vampire. But this is our task. In such a case the police, all the powers of society, are as helpless as the doctors. What bars or chains can hold a creature who can turn into a wolf or a bat?

HARKER: A wolf! Doctor Seward, those dogs howling! I told you they howl that way in Russia when wolves are about. And a bat . . . Renfield said there was a bat.

SEWARD: Well. What of it?

VAN HELSING: [*Reflectively.*] Your friend Renfield does not like the smell of wolfsbane.

SEWARD: But what in the world has your wolfsbane to do with all this?

VAN HELSING: A vampire cannot stand the smell of wolfsbane.

HARKER: You suspect that lunatic?

VAN HELSING: I suspect no one and everyone. . . . Tell me, who is this Count Dracula?

SEWARD: Dracula? We really know very little about him.

HARKER: When I was in Transylvania I heard of Castle Dracula. A famous Voivode Dracula who fought the Turks lived there centuries ago.

VAN HELSING: I will make inquiries by telegraph. No, but after all this Thing must be English. Or at least have died here. His lair must be near enough to this house for him to get back there before sunrise. [*To* SEWARD.] Oh, my friend, I have only the old beliefs with which to fight this monster that has the strength of twenty men, perhaps the accumulated wisdom and cunning of centuries.

HARKER: This all seems a nightmare. But I'm with you, Professor.

VAN HELSING: And you, Doctor Seward?

SEWARD: It all seems preposterous to me. But everyone else has failed. The case is in your hands at present.

VAN HELSING: [*Sternly.*] I need allies, not neutrals.

SEWARD: Very well, then, do what you will.

VAN HELSING: Good. Then bring your daughter here.

SEWARD: What are you going to do?

VAN HELSING: To set a trap. Miss Lucy is the bait.

HARKER: My God, we can't let you do that!

VAN HELSING: There's no other way. I believe this Thing knows that I plan to protect Miss Lucy. This will put it on its guard and the first moment she is alone it will no doubt try to get at her, for a vampire must have blood or its life in death ceases.

HARKER: No, I forbid this.

SEWARD: She's my daughter, and I consent. We'll show the Professor

Ticket stub from a 1931 production in Boston. (The Free Library of Philadelphia Theatre Collection)

ALEC HARFORD, THE MANIAC   JOAN COLBURN, THE GIRL   RAYMOND HUNTLEY, COUNT DRACULA   LESTER ALDEN, THE PROFESSOR

Newspaper cartoon of the touring company during its third Boston engagement. (The Free Library of Philadelphia Theatre Collection)

he's mistaken.

HARKER: You allow it only because you don't believe, and I do believe. My God, Doctor, I've heard that lunatic laugh . . . life-eating, you said he was, and you subject Lucy to that risk.

VAN HELSING: [*Interrupting harshly.*] I must be master here or I can do nothing! I must know in what form this Thing comes before I can plan how to stamp it out. Bring your daughter here.

> [SEWARD *turns and sees* HARKER *looking at him; stares at* HARKER. *There is a short pause, then* HARKER *reluctantly exits.* SEWARD *follows him.* VAN HELSING *thinks a moment, then looks about noting the positions of doors, furniture, etc. He then turns out lights. The room is dark except for the firelight.* VAN HELSING *moves into firelight, looks at divan, then walks back to door and turns, looking at divan, satisfying himself that the light from the fire is sufficient to see anything that happens on the divan. Opens curtains. Suddenly, the double doors open sharply and* VAN HELSING *starts violently; the* ATTENDANT *enters.*]

ATTENDANT: Beg pardon, sir. Is Doctor Seward here?

VAN HELSING: What do you want with him?

ATTENDANT: Ole Flycatcher's escaped again, sir.

VAN HELSING: Escaped, how?

ATTENDANT: Gor' blimme, out of the window. The door's still locked and I was in the corridor all the while. It's a drop of thirty feet to the stone flagging. That loonie's a bloomin' flyin' squirrel 'e is.

VAN HELSING: [*Commandingly.*] Say nothing to Doctor Seward at present. Nothing, do you hear? Now go.

[ATTENDANT *exits.* VAN HELSING *switches on lights again. Enter* LUCY, *supported by* HARKER *and* SEWARD.]

LUCY: Oh! Oh!

SEWARD: Lucy, you have nothing to fear.

[*They take her to divan.*]

VAN HELSING: I want you to lie down here, my dear.

LUCY: But, Doctor . . .

VAN HELSING: You trust me, do you not? [*She smiles weakly at him; nods. They place her on divan.*] I want you to lie here for just a little.

LUCY: But . . . I am so frightened.

VAN HELSING: Make your mind passive. Try not to think. Sleep if you can.

LUCY: I dare not sleep. It is when I sleep . . .

[HARKER *takes her hand.*]

VAN HELSING: [*Arranging her on divan, head on pillows, soothingly.*] I know, my dear. I know. I am going to cure you, with God's help.

LUCY: Oh, but, Father.

SEWARD: You must do as the Professor says. Come, Harker.

VAN HELSING: Come, Harker.

[VAN HELSING *leads* SEWARD *to the door.* SEWARD *exits.* HARKER *lingers and* VAN HELSING *calls him.* VAN HELSING *switches off lights as he and* HARKER *go out. No movement.* LUCY *closes her eyes. Low howl is heard outside . . . howl of a wolf. It is followed by a distant barking of dogs. Firelight grows dimmer.* DRACULA's *hand appears from back of couch, then his face.* LUCY *screams; swoons. When* LUCY *screams, ad libs offstage until* VAN HELSING *switches on lights.*]

HARKER: Lucy! Lucy!

SEWARD: Professor, what is it?

[VAN HELSING *enters, followed by* SEWARD *and* HARKER. VAN HELSING *switches on lights. They are just in front of door as a bat flies in the room from window to center, then out of the window.*]

As originally played on Broadway, this scene had Dracula appear over the divan in the form of a werewolf, a lifeless prop that often elicited more giggles than shrieks. Newspaper clippings indicate that the wolf was also used in Liveright's tours, but was written out of the script by the time the stock rights were released in 1930.

VAN HELSING: You saw?

SEWARD: God, what was that?

HARKER: Lucy, Lucy, speak to me!

VAN HELSING: Take her to her room, Harker, quickly.

[HARKER *carries* LUCY *to door as* DRACULA *enters. He looks about, his glance taking in everyone.*]

DRACULA: [*Mildly, sympathetically.*] The patient is better, I hope?

[RENFIELD *gives a wild laugh offstage right.* VAN HELSING, SEWARD *and* HARKER *turn.* RENFIELD *gives a second wild laugh.*]

CURTAIN

Lugosi was deluged with romantic fan attention during his stage run in *Dracula*. One especially persistent admirer was the actress Clara Bow, who succeeded in initiating a torrid affair. Raymond Huntley, who toured the east coast while Lugosi played in California, recalled that when Dracula was afoot the footlights, a certain number of women could always be expected to be "adventurous."

Act Two

LUCY's *boudoir. Window right rear, closed but curtains open. Chairs, small occasional table with toilet articles on it by window. Couch against wall up left center. Mirror on wall. Small stand, with flowers in vase, near couch. Doors, right, leading into bedroom, left, leading into hall. Arch left center.*

The next evening.

Dogs howling. As curtain rises, MAID *enters from bedroom, glances up at window over her left shoulder, takes a few steps, looks back over right shoulder, then to couch and takes newspaper. Sits on couch; reads newspaper. As she turns a page,* ATTENDANT *knocks on hall door.*

MAID: [*Starts.*] Who is that?

ATTENDANT: [*Enters; smiles at her.*] Excuse me, Miss. Did you 'appen to 'ave seen anything of the Guv'ner's pet looney? 'E's out again, 'e is.

MAID: [*Holding paper.*] And what would he be doing here? You'll not hold your job, you won't, if you can't keep that man safe and sound. Why, he gets out every night. [*She crosses toward bedroom door.*]

ATTENDANT: 'Ere, don't go, Miss.

MAID: Miss Lucy's asked for the evening paper.

[MAID *smiles as she goes off; indicates speedy return.* ATTENDANT *looks out of window and then looks under couch.* MAID *returns. Her line comes just as* ATTENDANT *bends over, causing him to jump back, frightened.*]

MAID: Well, have you found him?

ATTENDANT: No, I 'aven't. [*Confidentially.*] And I'll tell you, Miss, this job is fair gettin' on my nerves.

MAID: Your nerves? And what about *my* nerves? Isn't it enough to have dogs howling every night and foreign counts bobbing up out

The predatory profile: Raymond Huntley makes ready for a hideous repast.

Opposite: Bela Lugosi and Hazel Whitmore.

of the floor, and Miss Lucy taking on the way she does, with everybody having their veins drained of blood for her, and this Dutch Sherlock Holmes with the X-ray eyes about, without you letting that Renfield loose?

ATTENDANT: [*Grieved.*] I 'aven't let 'im loose. . . . Just now I 'ears a noise like a wolf 'owling. I opens 'is door with me key, and what do I see but 'is legs goin' through the window as though 'e was goin' to climb down that smooth wall. 'E ain't 'uman, 'e ain't.

MAID: Climb down the wall?

ATTENDANT: [*Gloomily.*] I don't expect no one to believe it, but I seen it, and w'ot's more, I grabbed 'old of 'is feet, I did.

MAID: [*Laughs unbelievingly.*] Climbing down, head first, like a bat?

ATTENDANT: Queer your mention of bats, for just as I got 'old of 'im, a big bat flies in the window and 'its me in the face.

MAID: [*Mysteriously.*] I know where that bat came from.

ATTENDANT: [*Startled.*] You do? Where?

Theda Fyler and Julio Brown as the Cockney maid and asylum attendant provided comic relief to nerve-wracked roadshow audiences.

MAID: Out of your belfry. [*Crosses to head of couch and arranges pillows, then to dresser.*]

ATTENDANT: No, Miss, it's Gawd's truth I'm tellin' yer . . . [*Look from her.*] . . . out that bat flies, and the looney is gone, but I 'eard 'im laugh, and Gawd, what a laugh. Blimme, but I'll catch it from the Guv'ner for this.

MAID: [*At dressing table.*] If you tell the Guvernor any such tales he'll shut you up with the looney.

ATTENDANT: Lor', Miss, but you're a smart one . . . that's just what I've been thinkin', and I daren't tell 'im what I see or what I 'eard. But 'e's 'armless, this bloke.

MAID: [*Ironically.*] Wouldn't hurt a fly, would he?

ATTENDANT: 'Urt a fly? Oh, no, not 'e. 'E only *eats* 'em. Why, 'e'd rather eat a few blue-bottles than a pound of the best steak, and what 'e does to spiders is a crime.

MAID: It seems to me somebody will be coming after *you* in a minute, you and your spiders.

ATTENDANT: I say, Miss. This is a queer neighborhood. [*Looking out of window.*] What a drop that is to the ground. [*Turns to her.*] You don't have to be afraid of burglars, do you? No way of getting up here unless they fly. . . . Don't you never feel a bit lonesome like, out there . . . [*Points to window.*] . . . on your nights off?

MAID: Just lately I have a bit. [*Looks toward window.*] I never noticed trees had such shadows before.

ATTENDANT: Well . . . if you feel you'd like a h'escort, Miss . . .

MAID: I'll not walk with you in your uniform. People might be taking me for one of your loonies.

ATTENDANT: [*Puts arm around her.*] In mufti, then, tomorrow night.

MAID: I say, you haven't wasted much time, have you?

ATTENDANT: I've 'ad my eye on you.

MAID: Better keep that eye on your looney, or you'll be looking for a new job. [ATTENDANT *tries to kiss her. She pushes him off and slaps him.*] Here, you. Buzz off. Your Guvernor will be in any minute. [*Gestures to door.*] Go find your looney.

ATTENDANT: Oh, orl right, but I've got somethin' 'ere that'll tempt 'im back to 'is room.

MAID: Why, what's that?

[*He fumbles in pocket. She comes up to him.*]

ATTENDANT: [*Takes white mouse by tail out of pocket; holds it in her face.*] This 'ere.

Lugosi's makeup, already weird on Broadway, was applied even more aggressively for the West Coast engagement.

MAID: [*Screams; climbs on chair; holds skirt.*] Take it away! Take it away!

·ATTENDANT: [*Mouse climbs up his arm to shoulder. To mouse:*] Come on, Cuthbert. We ain't too popular. [*Offended, walks off left with dignity, remarking from door:*] Some people 'ave *no* sense of humor.

SEWARD: [*Enters hastily from bedroom.*] What was that?

MAID: [*Puts down her skirt.*] Pardon, sir. He frightened me with that . . . that animal.

SEWARD: [*Agitated.*] Animal, what animal?

MAID: A white mouse, sir.

SEWARD: [*Relieved.*] You mustn't scream . . . not in this house . . . *now.*

MAID: I'm sorry, sir, but that nasty little beast . . .

SEWARD: You alarmed Miss Lucy so. She's dreadfully upset as it is by something in the paper.

MAID: Oh, do you mean about that Hampstead Horror, sir? The lady in white who gives chocolates to little children . . .

SEWARD: [*Interrupts impatiently.*] Never mind that, but I will not have Miss Lucy disturbed.

> [SEWARD *returns to bedroom. Dogs howl. Lights go out.* MAID *screams. Green spot comes up on* DRACULA *who stands in center of room.* MAID *screams again as she sees him.*]

DRACULA: [*Soothingly.*] Forgive me. My footfall is not heavy, and your rugs are soft.

MAID: It's all right, sir . . . but how did you come in?

DRACULA: [*Smiling.*] The door of this room was ajar, so I did not knock. How is Miss Lucy and her nervous prostration?

MAID: I think she's better, sir.

DRACULA: Ah, good. But the strain of Miss Lucy's illness has made you also ill.

MAID: How did you know, sir? But it's only a pain in my head that runs down into the neck.

DRACULA: [*Winningly.*] I can remove this pain.

MAID: I don't understand, sir.

DRACULA: Such pains yield readily to suggestion.

MAID: [*Raises arm slightly to shield herself.*] Excuse me, sir, but if it's hypnotism you mean, I'd rather have the pain.

DRACULA: Ah, you think of hypnotism as an ugly waving of arms and many passes. That is not my method. [*As he speaks he gestures quietly with his left hand and she stares at him, fascinated. Placing his left thumb against her forehead, he stares straight into her eyes. She makes a*

"You will obey each command that reaches you from my brain . . ." Raymond Huntley further domesticates the domestic, played by Theda Fyler. (The Harvard Theatre Collection)

feeble effort to remove his hand, then remains quiescent. He now speaks coldly, imperatively; turns her face front before speaking.] What is given can be taken away. From now on you have no pain. And you have no will of your own. Do you hear me?

MAID: [*Murmurs.*] I hear you.

DRACULA: When you awake you will not remember what I say. Doctor Seward ordered you today to sleep with your mistress every night in the same bed because of her bad dreams. Is it not so?

MAID: [*Murmurs.*] Yes, Master.

DRACULA: Your mistress is threatened by horror and by death, but I will save her. A man whose will is at cross purposes with mine has come to this house. I will crush him. Receive your orders. You hear me?

MAID: Yes, Master.

DRACULA: Hear and obey. From now on you will carry out any suggestion that reaches you from my brain instantly without question. When I will you to do a thing it shall be done. My call will reach you soon.

[*Green spot dims out slowly.* DRACULA *exits through window. Lights come on. Dogs howl outside.* MAID *looks up at window as* VAN HELSING *enters left. She starts when door shuts.*]

VAN HELSING: [*His face is paler. He looks drawn and weak. He carries box tied with string.*] You've not left your mistress alone?

MAID: Doctor Seward is with her, sir. [*Sways a little.*]

VAN HELSING: [*Looking at her keenly.*] What's wrong with you, my girl?

MAID: Nothing, sir.

VAN HELSING: You've just had a severe shock.

MAID: It's nothing, sir. I . . . I suddenly felt queer. [*Looks toward window.*] That's all. I can't remember anything.

VAN HELSING: Mr. Harker has just arrived. Ask Doctor Seward to come here. Remain with Miss Lucy yourself.

MAID: Yes, sir. She's dreadfully upset, sir.

VAN HELSING: Upset over what?

MAID: It's in the evening paper, sir. About the Hampstead Horror.

[VAN HELSING *motions* MAID *to silence.*] Yes, sir.

VAN HELSING: [*Shaken.*] Oh, God, she has seen it!

[MAID *goes into bedroom.* HARKER *enters left.*]

Given the indelible mark he made on the role, it is surprising that Bela Lugosi's performance was not greeted with universal enthusiasm by the critics. Alexander Woollcott, in *The World*, made note of the actor's "incongruous accent," which audiences might associate with "lovable and threadbare music masters." Brooks Atkinson called Lugosi's acting "a little too deliberate and confident." The *New York Post* compared him to "an operatically inclined but cheerless mortician." *The Herald Tribune* complained that Lugosi's Dracula was a "rigid hobgoblin," more window mannequin than suave demon. Little did these critics realize that they were witnessing the birth of one of the most instantly recognizable and imitated characterizations in theatrical history.

Margot Lester as Lucy.

Opposite: Another night, another neck. Bela Lugosi eagerly explores the ample charms of Hazel Whitmore.

HARKER: [*Worried.*] Everything just the same? [VAN HELSING *nods.* HARKER *closes door.*] When I leave this house even for a few hours I dread what I . . . I dread what I may find when I come back.

VAN HELSING: And well you may, my friend. [*He places box on table under mirror.*]

HARKER: God must have sent you here to help us. Without you there'd be no hope. And this morning, Professor, when you opened your veins to revive Lucy again . . .

VAN HELSING: It was the least I could do . . . for my lack of foresight was responsible for this attack.

HARKER: Don't say that.

VAN HELSING: Her maid slept with her . . . and yet we found the wolfsbane thrown off the bed to the floor.

HARKER: She was so weak, so pale, the two little wounds opened fresh again . . .

VAN HELSING: [*With gesture to box.*] I have prepared a stronger defense. But our main task is not defense, but attack. What have you found in London?

HARKER: A lot, but heaven knows what it means or whether it's any use.

VAN HELSING: I, too, have had news of which I can make nothing.

SEWARD: [*Enters.*] Ah, John, back from town.

HARKER: Yes. [*Sits.*]

VAN HELSING: We must try to piece together what we have learned today. [*Producing telegram of several sheets.*] My colleague in Bucharest wires that the Dracula family has been extinct . . . for five hundred years.

SEWARD: Can the Count be an impostor?

VAN HELSING: [*Referring to telegram.*] The castle he calls his own is a desolate ruin near the border. It was built, as you said, Harker, by the terrible Voivode Dracula, who was said to have had dealings with evil spirits. He was the last of his race. But for many generations the peasants have believed the Castle Dracula inhabited by a vampire.

HARKER: Then it must be he . . .

VAN HELSING: [*Shakes head; puts telegram back in pocket.*] My friends, I am bewildered.

SEWARD: But surely this confirms your suspicions. I was incredulous till I saw that creature hovering over Lucy . . .

VAN HELSING: A vampire from Transylvania cannot be in England.

SEWARD: But why?

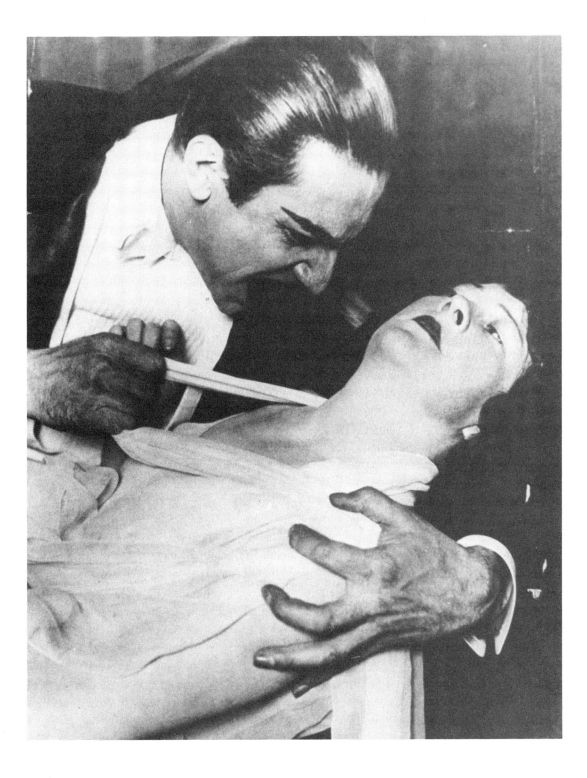

TREAT YOURSELF TO A STRANGE INTERLUDE *of* HORROR!

OHIO TONIGHT

LAST WEEKS

MATS. WED. & SAT.

DRACULA

The MOST AMAZING, NERVE TINGLING DRAMA *in* THE HISTORY *of* THE ENGLISH SPEAKING STAGE

☞ YOU MAY BE SORRY IF YOU COME. BUT YOU'LL REGRET IT FOREVER, IF YOU DON'T!!

EMERGENCY HOSPITAL IN THE FOYER, DOCTOR AND NURSE IN CONSTANT ATTENDANCE

SUMMER SHOWS START SOON — SEASON RESERVATIONS NOW!

Cleveland audiences were suffi-ciently enamored of Dracula to persuade Horace Liveright to assemble a special company for an extended run at the Ohio Theatre in the spring of 1929. Below, Marion Swayne as Lucy is menaced by Howard Sinclair, the only stage Dracula of the time to sport a Mephistophelian goatee.

VAN HELSING: Because, as I have told you, the vampire must rest by day in the earth in which the corpse it inhabits was buried.

HARKER: [*Rises.*] In the earth.

VAN HELSING: The vampire must return to its burial place by sunrise.

HARKER: [*Excited.*] I found today that Dracula arrived at the Croydon airdrome in a three-engined German plane, on March sixth.

SEWARD: March the sixth? Three days before Mina first was taken ill.

HARKER: This plane had made a nonstop flight from Sekely in Transylvania. It left just after sunset. It arrived two hours before dawn. It carried only the Count and six packing cases.

VAN HELSING: Did you learn what was in those cases?

HARKER: He told the customs people he wanted to see whether Transylvania plants would grow in a foreign climate in their native soil.

VAN HELSING: Soil? What was in those boxes?

HARKER: Just plain dirt. He left in a lorry, with the six coffinlike boxes, before sunrise.

VAN HELSING: Oh, God, yes, before sunrise. The King of Vampires, my friends. [*Crosses between* SEWARD *and* HARKER.] This creature is the terrible Voivode Dracula himself! In his satanic pride and contempt, he even uses his own name. For who could suspect? For five hundred years he has been fettered to his castle because he must sleep by day in his graveyard. Five centuries pass. The airplane is invented. His chance has come, for now he can cross Europe in a single night. He prepared six coffins filled with the earth in which he must rest by day. He leaves his castle after sunset. By dawn he is in London and safe in one of his cases—a great risk, but he has triumphed. He has reached London with its teeming millions, with its "opportunity," as he said . . .

SEWARD: God protect my Lucy!

HARKER: [*To* VAN HELSING, *new tone.*] I saw the estate agent from whom he bought Carfax here and got the address of four old houses he has leased in different parts of London.

VAN HELSING: One of his coffin retreats is in each of those houses.

SEWARD: Two heavy boxes were delivered at Carfax the day after he took possession.

VAN HELSING: He has scattered them, for safety. If we can find all six, we can destroy him.

SEWARD: But how?

VAN HELSING: His native earth will no longer receive his unclean

An example of a typical press release issued by Horace Liveright Theatrical Productions: "While Horace Liveright doesn't believe in the supernatural nor the manifestations of ectoplasm, so many strange happenings have occurred to his production of *Dracula* that Mr. Liveright is beginning to wonder. In New Haven, the night of the opening there, the stage manager, a man noted for his coolness, and hitherto untouched by such malady as stagefright, was seized, so the Liveright office asserts, by a sudden attack of aphasia. His mind, temporarily, became a blank. Signals from the stage manager's desk to the men in the flies of the theatre went 'dead.' Since the opening in New York, enough disturbing things of a like nature have transpired that the Liveright staff and players have become highly nervous. Even the understudy has become panicky and given in her notice. Was it the spirit of Dracula, or of the press agent? Draw your own conclusions."

form if each box is sanctified with holy water.

HARKER: Then we must get at those boxes, tear them open one by one. If we find him, then in God's name, Professor, I demand that my hand shall drive the stake into this devil's heart and send his soul to hell!

[SEWARD *motions no noise because of* LUCY.]

VAN HELSING: Your plan is too dangerous.

SEWARD: But why? These attacks on Lucy continue. Are we to delay while my child is dying?

HARKER: No, not for a moment.

VAN HELSING: Patience, my friends. This creature is more than mortal. His cunning is the growth of the ages. How if we find five of his boxes and close them against him, and cannot find the sixth?

SEWARD: Well?

VAN HELSING: Then he will bury himself in his last refuge, where we can never find him and sleep until we are all dead.

HARKER: Then Lucy will be safe.

VAN HELSING: For her life, yes . . . but his unclean kiss has claimed her for his own. When she dies she will become as he is, a foul thing of the night. The vampire can wait. No, my friends, there is only one way to save her from him . . . to destroy him.

SEWARD: You're right, as always.

VAN HELSING: We have one great advantage . . . by day he is a coffined corpse . . . of our search by day he can know nothing, if we leave no traces.

HARKER: God, this delay!

VAN HELSING: We must make the round of his houses and find all six boxes, without his knowledge, and *then* we act.

SEWARD: But what about the caretakers or servants?

VAN HELSING: All the houses will be empty. The vampire plays a lone hand.

[*Maniacal laugh heard behind curtains of window.* SEWARD *crosses quickly to window.*]

SEWARD: Renfield!

[*He grabs* RENFIELD *by arm and throws him into room.* RENFIELD *laughs cunningly.*]

VAN HELSING: He's been here all the time we've been talking.

SEWARD: Did you hear what we were saying, man?

Courtney White made a brooding stock-circuit Dracula in 1930 and 1931. (The Free Library of Philadelphia Theatre Collection)

Victor Jory spooked 1930 audiences with a highly stylized, almost expressionistic makeup. His Minneapolis victim, seen here, was Allison Dwyer. Later the same year, Jory recreated his characterization of the Count for the Pasadena Community Playhouse.

This play is not the play of the same name which ran in London, and which has been circulated but not produced on the Continent. It was written by arrangement with Mrs. Bram-Stoker, the owner of the copyright of the book, and Mr. Hamilton Deane, author of the English version, but contains only a few lines from the English version which it now supercedes.

This MSS. has not hitherto been offered or shown outside the United States.

This play was first produced September 20th, 1927, and is now (May 1929) still running, and booked well into next season. Its business record has been as follows: (engagements one week unless otherwise stated)

Tryout, 15 performances	8,314.50
Fulton, New York (33 weeks)	342,542.50
Los Angeles, 8 weeks, Coast Company	62,018.00
San Francisco, 4 weeks, Coast Company	46,062.00
Atlantic City	13,449.00
Bronx	15,805.00
Boston, 3 weeks	40,513.00
Brooklyn	16,216.00
Washington	13,710.00
Baltimore	10,434.00
Philadelphia, 6 weeks	91,480.00
Buffalo	9,867.00
Cleveland	16,096.00
Cincinnatti	13,441.00
Detroit, 2 weeks	25,937.00
Brooklyn	14,433.00
Shubert Riviera, New York	11,330.00
Windsor Bronx	13,535.00
Newark	17,843.00
Flatbush	12,747.00
Jackson Heights	16,736.00
Pittsburgh, 2 weeks	30,033.00
Toronto	12,171.00
Chicago (5 weeks still running)	67,100.00
Cleveland special company, 5 weeks	40,604.00
No. 2 Company	37,898.00

Total gross September 20th, 1927 to
May 4th, 1929 . . . . $1,000,315.00

Another coast company now opening in
San Francisco.(?)Stock rights and film
rights not yet released.

RENFIELD: Yes, I heard . . . something . . . enough . . . [*With gestures to* SEWARD *and* HARKER.] Be guided by what he says. [*Points to* VAN HELSING.] It is your only hope. . . . It is her only hope. [*Crosses to* VAN HELSING.] It is *my* only hope. [*Falls on knees before* VAN HELSING.] Save my soul! Save my soul! I am weak. You are strong. I am crazy. You are sane. You are good and he is evil.

VAN HELSING: [*Impressively.*] I will save you, Renfield, but you must tell me what you know. Everything.

RENFIELD: [*Rises.*] Know? What should I know? I don't know anything. [*Taps head.*] You say I'm mad and Doctor Seward will tell you about that. You mustn't pay any attention to anything I say.

SEWARD: We can't waste time with this fellow. I'll have him taken away. [*Crosses to bell.*]

RENFIELD: [*To* SEWARD.] Fool, fool, and I thought you were wise! The whole world is mad just now, and if you want help you must come to a madman to get it. [*Little laugh, cunningly.*] But I'll not give it to you, I'm afraid. [*Turns to window.*] A wise madman will obey him who is strong and not the weak.

VAN HELSING: [*Moves to him fiercely.*] Him? Whom do you mean?

RENFIELD: Need we mention names among friends? Come, Professor, be reasonable. What have I got to gain by being on your side? The Doctor keeps me shut up all day, and if I'm good he gives me a little sugar to spread out for my flies, but on the other hand, if I serve *him* . . . [*Points to window.*]

VAN HELSING: [*Sharply, taking him by coat.*] The blood is the life, eh, Renfield? [*Dragging him again.*] What have you to do with Count Dracula?

RENFIELD: [*Convulsed with terror.*] Dracula! [*Drawing himself up defiantly.*] I never even heard the name before!

VAN HELSING: You are lying!

RENFIELD: Madmen, Professor, lack the power to discriminate between truth and falsehood . . . [*Breaks away.*] . . . so I take no offense at what most men would consider an affront. [*Crosses to* SEWARD.] Send me away! I asked you to before and you wouldn't. If you only knew what has happened since then. I dare not tell you more. I dare not! I should die in torment if I betrayed . . .

VAN HELSING: Doctor Seward will send you away if you speak.

SEWARD: Yes, Renfield. [RENFIELD *moans.*] I offer you your soul in exchange for what you know.

RENFIELD: God will not damn a poor lunatic's soul. God knows the

One of the strangest bits of casting for the title role of *Dracula* was the tennis superstar Bill Tilden, who had a dark personal attraction to the part and played it in a series of one-night stand engagements around 1930—much to John Balderston's disapproval. In the 1940s, Tilden returned to the predatory role—weirdly, in the wake of two recent convictions for molesting young boys. The revival was a disaster, and ruined the troubled Tilden financially. He died in 1953.

Earnings sheet for Dracula, *1927–1929. By the following year, the gross recipts would double.*

The New York Telegraph's critic Burton Davis likened *Dracula* to the excesses of a freak circus. "As a drama it is about on a par with a sword-swallowing act," Davis wrote the morning after the opening. "There are some—and I am one of them—who get no sensual satisfaction out of such self-torture as *Dracula* offers; it leaves me, to tell the gospel truth, quite unmoved, with a normal pulse, an unhurried heart, a brow unspangled by perspiration and a mind still bored. But all around me I hear the gasps and chuckles of pained delight with which some of Horace Liveright's most famous literary attaches were greeting the hocus-pocus on the stage." Citing psychiatric testimony that one person out of four enjoyed morbid thrills, "and since the population, fixed and transient, of New York, is large, you can figure out for yourself how long this might last. It will be a great road-show, too. It should run here until a new freak displaces it."

devil is too strong for us who have weak minds. But send me away ... I want you to promise, Doctor Seward!

SEWARD: If you will speak.

VAN HELSING: Come, Renfield.

RENFIELD: [*Pause. Looks at* SEWARD, VAN HELSING, HARKER, *and* SEWARD *again, then speaks as a sane man.*] Then I will tell you. Count Dracula is ... [*Bat comes in window; flies out again.* RENFIELD *rushes to window with arms outstretched, screaming.*] Master! Master, I didn't say anything! I told them nothing. I'm loyal to you. I am your slave.

[SEWARD *and* HARKER *rush to window.*]

SEWARD: [*Looking out window.*] There's a big bat flying in a circle. It's gone.

HARKER: What's that, just passing that small shrub? It looks like a big gray dog.

VAN HELSING: Are you sure it was a dog?

HARKER: Well, it might easily be a wolf. Oh, but that's nonsense. Our nerves are making us see things.

VAN HELSING: Come, Renfield. What were you about to say?

RENFIELD: Nothing, nothing.

[LUCY *comes in from bedroom with newspaper.*]

LUCY: Professor ... have you seen what's in this ...

VAN HELSING: Miss Lucy, give it to ...

RENFIELD: [*Crosses to her.*] Are you Miss Seward?

LUCY: I am.

[SEWARD *moves closer to her; indicates* HARKER *to ring bell.*]

RENFIELD: Then in the name of the merciful and compassionate God, leave this place at once!

[*She turns to him.* VAN HELSING *motions silence to others.*]

LUCY: But this is my home. Nothing would induce me to leave.

RENFIELD: [*Sane.*] Oh, that's true. You wouldn't go if they tried to drag you away, would you? It's too late. What a fool I am. I shall be punished for this and it can't do any good. It's too late. [*In tone of pity.*] You are so young, so beautiful, so pure. Even I have decent feelings sometimes, and I must tell you, and if you don't go your soul will pay for it. You're in the power of ... [*Bat flies in window and out.* RENFIELD *rushes to window and screams.* SEWARD *moves toward couch.* HARKER *crosses to* LUCY *to protect her.*] The Master is at hand!

> [RENFIELD *crosses back on knees.* ATTENDANT *appears at door.*]

SEWARD: Butterworth!

> [SEWARD *helps* RENFIELD *up, then* ATTENDANT *grasps him and takes him to door.*]

RENFIELD: [*At door.*] Goodbye, Miss Seward. Since you will not heed my warning, I pray God that I may never see your face again.

> [*He exits with* ATTENDANT.]

Bela at bay: Right to left, Edward Van Sloan, Terrence Neill, Lugosi, Herbert Bunston, Bernard Jukes.

LUCY: What did he mean, Professor? What did he mean? Why did he say that?

[*She goes off into bedroom, in hysterics.* HARKER *follows her.*]

SEWARD: That crazy thing in league with the devil; horrible, and Lucy already upset by something in the paper.

VAN HELSING: Go in and get that paper from her.

SEWARD: Whatever it is, she keeps on reading that article again and again.

VAN HELSING: Take it away from her, man, and come back to me. [*Places hand on forehead as if faint.*]

SEWARD: Don't overdo it, Van Helsing. God knows where we should be if you went under. After a transfusion operation, at your age you really ought to be in bed ... the loss of so much blood is serious.

VAN HELSING: I never felt more fit in my life.

SEWARD: I only ask you not to overestimate your strength now, when we lean on you. . . . [*As he exits.*] Feeling fit, are you? Just look at yourself in the glass.

[VAN HELSING, *alone, registers as tired and exhausted, and walks slowly across room, looking at his drawn face in mirror.* DRACULA, *with stealthy tread, in evening dress and cloak as before, enters from window and walks slowly to directly behind* VAN HELSING.]

VAN HELSING: [*Looking at himself, touching face, shakes head.*] The devil.

DRACULA: Come. [VAN HELSING *turns suddenly to him and looks back into the mirror.*] Not as bad as that. [*Suave, cold, ironical.*]

VAN HELSING: [*Long look in mirror, then turns to* DRACULA. *Controlling himself with difficulty.*] I did not hear you, Count.

DRACULA: I am often told that I have a light footstep.

VAN HELSING: I was looking in the mirror. Its reflection covers the whole room, but I cannot see . . .

[*Pause. He turns to mirror.* DRACULA, *face convulsed by fury, picks up small vase with flowers from stand, smashes mirror, pieces of mirror and vase tumbling to floor.* VAN HELSING *steps back; looks at* DRACULA *with loathing and terror.*]

DRACULA: [*Recovering composure.*] Forgive me, I dislike mirrors. They are the playthings of man's vanity. . . . And how's the fair patient?

VAN HELSING: [*Meaningly.*] The diagnosis presents difficulties.

DRACULA: I feared it might, my friend.

VAN HELSING: Would you care to see what I have prescribed for my patient?

DRACULA: Anything that you prescribe for Miss Lucy has the greatest interest for me.

[VAN HELSING *crosses to table to get box.* DRACULA *crosses, meets* VAN HELSING *coming back with box.* VAN HELSING *deliberately turns away from him, goes to small table right of arch, turns front as he opens pocketknife and, in cutting string of parcel, cuts his finger. He gives slight exclamation of pain; holds up finger covered with blood.* DRACULA *starts for* VAN HELSING *with right hand raised, then keeping control with difficulty, turns away so as not to see blood.* VAN HELSING *stares at him a moment, then walks up and sticks bleeding finger in front of him.*]

VAN HELSING: The prescription is a most unusual one.

[DRACULA, *baring teeth, makes sudden snap at finger.* VAN HELSING *turns away quickly; ties handkerchief around it.* DRACULA *again regains poise with an effort.*]

DRACULA: The cut is not deep . . . I . . . looked.

VAN HELSING: [*Opening parcel.*] No, but it will serve. Here is my medicine for Miss Lucy. [DRACULA *comes up to* VAN HELSING, *who quickly holds handful of wolfsbane up to his face.* DRACULA *leaps back, face distorted with rage and distress, shielding himself with cloak. Putting wolfsbane back in box.*] You do not care for the smell?

DRACULA: You are a wise man, Professor . . . for one who has not lived even a single lifetime.

VAN HELSING: You flatter me, Count.

DRACULA: But not wise enough to return to Holland at once, now that you have learned what you have learned.

VAN HELSING: [*Shortly.*] I preferred to remain. [*Meaningly.*] Even though a certain lunatic here attempted to kill me.

DRACULA: [*Smiling.*] Lunatics are difficult. They do not do what they are told. They even try to betray their benefactors. But when servants fail to obey orders, the Master must carry them out for himself.

VAN HELSING: [*Grimly.*] I anticipated as much.

DRACULA: [*Gazing at him intently.*] In the past five hundred years,

Horace Liveright imported Hamilton Deane's gimmick of stationing the uniformed nurse in the lobby for all performances. One young ticket buyer at the Fulton Theatre named Bill Schloss was highly impressed by the ballyhoo. Later, as horror movie maven William Castle, he would introduce similarly hokey publicity stunts for films like *Macabre*, *The Tingler*, and *House on Haunted Hill*.

Disappearing act: this vanishing trick didn't occur on stage, but made an effective publicity photo nonetheless. (The Free Library of Philadelphia Theatre Collection)

Dracula is repelled by the power of the Host. According to John Balderston, the archbishop of Detroit was especially charmed by this scene.

Professor, those who have crossed my path have all died, and some not pleasantly. [*Continues to gaze at* VAN HELSING; *lifts his arm slowly; says with terrible emphasis and force.*] Come . . . here. [VAN HELSING *pales, staggers, then slowly takes three steps toward* DRACULA. *Very slight pause as* VAN HELSING *attempts to regain control of himself, then takes another step toward* DRACULA; *pauses, places hand to brow, then completely regains control of himself and looks away.*] Ah, your will is strong. Then I must come to you. [*Advances to* VAN HELSING, *who takes out of breast pocket small velvet bag.* DRACULA *stops.*] More medicine, Professor?

VAN HELSING: More effective than wolfsbane, Count.

DRACULA: Indeed? [*Starts for* VAN HELSING's *throat.* VAN HELSING *holds bag out toward him.* DRACULA's *face becomes convulsed with terror and he retreats left before* VAN HELSING, *who follows him.*] Sacrilege.

VAN HELSING: [*Continuing to advance.*] I have a dispensation.

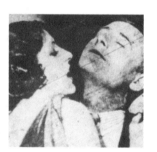

Margot Lester introduces Terrence Neill to a new-fangled erogenous zone.

[VAN HELSING *has cut him off from the door and remorselessly presses him toward window.* DRACULA, *livid with rage and snarling, backs out of the window. As* DRACULA *is just outside the window he spreads his cape like a bat and gives a long satirical laugh as he makes exit.* VAN HELSING *almost collapses; puts bag back in pocket; crosses himself; mops perspiration from brow with handkerchief. A shot is heard.* VAN HELSING *leaps up; rushes to window. Bat circles almost into his face. He staggers back.* SEWARD *hurries in, carrying newspaper.*]

SEWARD: God, Van Helsing, what was that? [*Dropping newspaper on table.*]

VAN HELSING: A revolver shot. It came as a relief. That at least is something human.

SEWARD: Who broke the mirror?

VAN HELSING: I.

[HARKER *enters.*]

HARKER: Sorry if I startled you. I saw that infernal bat around this side of the house. I couldn't resist a shot.

SEWARD: Did you hit it?

HARKER: Why, I . . .

VAN HELSING: The bullet was never made, my friend, that could harm *that* bat. *My* weapons are stronger.

HARKER: What do you mean?

An "unclean" Margot Lester recoils from Terrence Neill's embrace.

VAN HELSING: Dracula has been here.

SEWARD: Good God!

HARKER: How did he get in?

VAN HELSING: You ask how the Vampire King, during the hours of night, the hours that are his, comes and goes? As the wind, my friend, as he pleases. He came to kill me. ↗ . . . But I carry a power stronger than his.

HARKER: What power?

VAN HELSING: I expected an attack. I secured a dispensation from the Cardinal. I have with me . . . [*Crosses himself.*] . . . the Host. [HARKER *crosses himself.*] He came. I proved my case if it needed proof. The mirror does not reflect this *man that was*, who casts no shadow. See, I cut my finger, *it* leapt at the blood, but before the sacred wafer *it* fled.

SEWARD: Lucy must not know.

VAN HELSING: [*Gently, worried.*] Miss Lucy knows . . . more than you think.

HARKER: How can she? If she knew, she'd tell me.

VAN HELSING: As these attacks continue she comes more and more under his power. There is a mystic link between them. [SEWARD *sighs.*] Oh, it is hard to bear, but you must face it. It may be that he can already learn what passes in her mind. And so Miss Lucy must not be told that we know about earth boxes . . . for he may learn . . . whatever she knows.

[LUCY *enters.*]

When given the finger, a vampire reacts with understandable outrage. From the 1928 West Coast tour.

SEWARD: But Professor, that would mean that Lucy is in collusion with this creature. That's impossible....

[LUCY *crosses to table; takes newspaper.*]

VAN HELSING: No, no, Miss Lucy, you must not.
HARKER: Lucy, what's in this paper that's upset you?
LUCY: [*Hands newspaper to* HARKER.] Read it, John.

[HARKER *takes newspaper; reads.* VAN HELSING *moves as if to stop him, then checks himself.*]

VAN HELSING: No, Harker, no.
LUCY: Read it!

[LUCY *sits on couch. They all listen.*]

HARKER: [*Reading.*] "The Hampstead Horror. Further attacks on small children, committed after dark by a mysterious and beautiful woman in Hampstead, are reported today. Narratives of three small girls, all under ten years of age, tally in essential details. Each child speaks of a beautiful lady in white who gave her chocolates, enticed her to some secluded corner and there kissed and fondled her and bit her slightly in the throat." [*He looks at* SEWARD *and* LUCY.]
LUCY: Go on.
HARKER: [*Reading.*] "The wounds are trivial. The children suffered no other harm and do not seem to have been frightened. Indeed, one small girl told her mother she hoped she might see the beautiful lady again."

[*He turns to* LUCY. SEWARD *takes paper from* HARKER.]

VAN HELSING: So soon ... so soon.

[HARKER *and* SEWARD *look at each other.*]

SEWARD: You know what has been happening, Lucy? [LUCY *nods.*]
HARKER: Professor Van Helsing knows, too, Lucy, and he knows how to protect you.
LUCY: Is it not too late?
VAN HELSING: No, Miss Lucy, it is not too late.
SEWARD: These poor innocent children ...
VAN HELSING: [*To* SEWARD.] You think Count Dracula ...
LUCY: [*Shudders.*] Not that name.
VAN HELSING: You think the Werewolf has done this too?

Above: Lugosi won the 1931 film role against stiff competition. Opposite: Publicity page from a British film magazine.

Dracula

The Vampire Thriller, adapted from Bram Stoker's famous novel
(Universal)

Dracula (a vampire), who has apparently died 500 years before, and is one of the terrifying "undead," arrives at the Seward home to pay his respects to Mina (Helen Chandler), her sweetheart, John Harker (David Manners), and Dr. Van Hesling (Edward Van Sloan). Dracula plans to get them in his power, but Dr. Van Hesling suspects him.

Dracula (Bela Lugosi), who can turn himself into a bat, a wolf, or a cloud of mist at night-time, terrifies Mina, who tells Harker of her horrible experiences.

(On left)
Though Dracula has almost succeeded in placing Van Hesling under an hypnotic spell, his power is destroyed when the scientist holds a cross before his eyes. As the sun rises Dracula, powerless in the day, sinks into insensibility, and his pursuers send him to a permanent death.

CARL
LAEMMLE
PRESENTA

"DRACULA"

SUPERPRODUCCION
UNIVERSAL
TOTALMENTE HABLADA
EN ESPAÑOL

Two film adaptations of the Deane-Balderston play were released by Universal in 1931: an elegant, Spanish-language version starring Carlos Villarias as the vampire, and the more familiar (and pedestrian) adaptation directed by Tod Browning.

SEWARD: Of course, in the form of a woman. Who else could it be?

VAN HELSING: It is worse. Far worse.

HARKER: Worse? What do you mean?

[LUCY *is motionless, her face frozen in horror.*]

VAN HELSING: Miss Lucy knows.

LUCY: The woman in white . . . is Mina.

HARKER: Mina. But she's dead, Lucy.

LUCY: She has joined . . . the Master.

SEWARD: Oh, God, have pity on us all. [*Drops newspaper on chair.*]

VAN HELSING: My dear Miss Lucy, I will not ask you how you know. After tonight no more little children will meet the woman in white. She will remain at rest . . . in the tomb where you laid her. And her soul, released from this horror, will be with God.

LUCY: How can you do this?

VAN HELSING: Do not ask me.

LUCY: [*Takes hold of* VAN HELSING'*s arm.*] Professor, if you can save Mina's soul after her death, can you save mine?

HARKER: Oh, Lucy! [*Sitting on couch, arm around her.*]

VAN HELSING: [*Takes her hand.*] I will save you. In God's name, I swear it. And He has given me a sign . . . in this room tonight.

LUCY: Then promise me one thing. Whatever you plan to do, whatever you know, do not tell me. [*Turns to* HARKER.] Not even if I beg *you* to tell me, swear that you will not, now, while I am still yours, while I am myself, promise it.

HARKER: I promise it. [*Takes her in his arms; tries to kiss her.*]

LUCY: [*Breaks from him, horrified.*] No, no, John! You mustn't kiss me. Promise that you never will, not even if I beg you to.

HARKER: I promise.

VAN HELSING: My dear Miss Lucy, from tonight on one of us will be awake all night, here in this room, next to your bedroom, with your door open.

LUCY: [*Murmurs.*] You are so good.

VAN HELSING: Yes, and I will make the room safe for you. Your maid will be with you. [HARKER *talks to* LUCY *on couch while* VAN HELSING *takes handful of wolfsbane.*] Doctor, rub these over the window in the little room there. See, like this. [*He starts rubbing around edge of window.*] Rub it around the sashes and especially above the lock. [SEWARD *watches* VAN HELSING *rubbing, then takes wolfsbane from* VAN HELSING *quickly, and goes out through arch.* VAN HELSING *turns, goes to table and takes out wreath of wolfsbane.*] See, I have made this

The Mexican ingenue Lupita Tovar made a fetching heroine in the Spanish-language Dracula.

wreath that you must wear around your neck tonight. While you wear this those ... dreams ... cannot come to you. [*Hangs wolfsbane around her neck. Takes out of pocket crucifix on cord, which he also hangs around her neck.*] Swear to me that you will not take these off.

LUCY: I promise.

VAN HELSING: Swear it on the cross.

LUCY: [*Kisses cross.*] I swear it!

[VAN HELSING *crosses toward door.*]

HARKER: Professor, surely the Host is more powerful than this wolfsbane.

VAN HELSING: Of course.

HARKER: Then leave the Host with her ... nothing can harm her then.

VAN HELSING: No, the Host cannot be used where there has been pollution. [*Screams off left.*] What is it?

[ATTENDANT *enters left.* MAID *comes in from bedroom;* SEWARD *enters from arch.*]

ATTENDANT: It's Renfield, sir.

SEWARD: Why haven't you got him locked up?

ATTENDANT: Because he's barred himself in, sir. He got hold of one of the patients. He had her by the throat.

[*He exits.* LUCY *rises.*]

VAN HELSING: Ah ... human blood now! [*Starting.*] Come, Seward! Come, Harker!

SEWARD: I should have had him sent away!

[MAID *crosses to* LUCY. VAN HELSING *and* SEWARD *exit.* HARKER *hesitates, then follows them off.* HARKER *ad libs during exit,* "It's all right, Lucy. I'll be right back," *etc.*]

LUCY: John ... [*To* MAID.] Don't you leave me, too.

MAID: Of course I won't, Miss Lucy. It's nothing but a quarrel among the patients. Mr. Harker will be back soon. [MAID *places her on couch.* LUCY *swoons.* MAID *gets smelling salts.*] Here, Miss Lucy. [DRACULA's *face appears back of tapestry on rear wall; disappears after a count of eight or nine.* MAID *steps down right, gets message, then returns. Puts salts back on dresser; crosses to* LUCY.] These evil-smelling flowers have made you faint. [*Takes crucifix and wreath from around*

Louis Cline, General Manager of Horace Liveright Theatrical Productions, who masterminded the Dracula *ballyhoo in the late 1920s.*

Without Fear of Contradiction
The Most Gripping—Thrilling—Exciting—Amazing of All
Mystery Plays

Horace Liveright presents
The **Sensational**
Vampire Mystery Play

DRACULA

dramatized by
Hamilton Dean and
John L. Balderston
from
Bram Stoker's famous novel

ONE YEAR IN
NEW YORK
FOUR YEARS IN
ENGLAND

Staged by Ira Hards

Bela Lugosi and Carroll Borland in Mark of the Vampire *(1935)*

LUCY'*s neck, throws them on floor; crosses two steps down right. Another message comes to her. Puts hand to head, turns slowly, looks at window, steps toward couch.*] It is so close, Madam. A little air . . . [*Turns to window.* LUCY *moans again.* MAID *pulls back latch; opens window. As window opens, clouds of mist roll in. Steps down. Gets message. Count eight. Switches out lights, then exits into bedroom. The stage is now dark. Dogs without, far and near, howl in terror. A gauze curtain comes down and a green light dims up covering the couch and center of the stage, revealing* DRACULA *standing center with back to audience, hands outstretched to resemble a large bat. As he moves up a few steps,* LUCY *slowly rises from couch and falls into his arms. A long kiss and then, as she falls back on his right arm, he bares her throat and starts to bite her as:*]

CURTAIN

Actress Carroll Borland, invited by Lugosi to perform in a condensed version of *Dracula* on the vaudeville circuit in 1932, recalled how the mood of this scene was hilariously shattered when a woman in the front row, oblivious to the performance, announced loudly to her companion that "I always fry mine in butter." Lugosi had to cover his face with his cape to keep from laughing. Borland also remembered the evening Lugosi added a truly spine-chilling touch— by dropping an ice cube down her negligee.

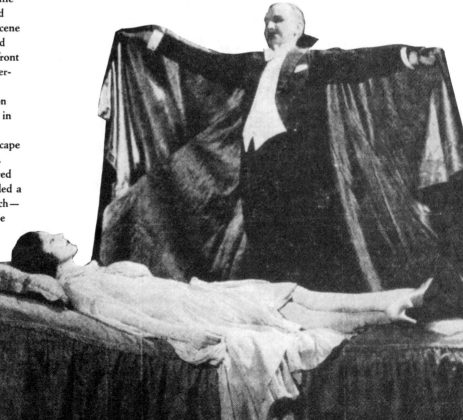

Bela Lugosi prepares to make an unholy feast of the producer's real-life girlfriend (Dorothy Peterson).

The passionate kiss between Dracula and his victim was notably omitted from the 1931 film version. Lugosi's onstage lovemaking was apparently so "hot" as to be downright dangerous. While appearing on Broadway in *The Red Poppy* with Estelle Winwood in 1926, the vampire-to-be embraced his leading lady so enthusiastically that he actually cracked two of her ribs.

Opposite: Raymond Huntley spreads a malignant influence over the sleeping Lucy, played here by Joan Colburn.

Act Three

The library. Thirty-two hours later, shortly before sunrise.

A stake and hammer are on desk. Dogs howl. Curtains move as if someone is entering window. Then chair back of desk, which is turned upstage, moves around, facing front. After a moment, VAN HELSING *enters with* SEWARD. VAN HELSING *paces up and down;* SEWARD *sits at desk. The center doors are flung open and the* ATTENDANT *comes in.*

VAN HELSING: What is it?

ATTENDANT: [*To* VAN HELSING.] Anybody w'ot wants my job, sir, can 'ave it.

[SEWARD *rouses himself.*]

SEWARD: What's the matter?

ATTENDANT: I knows what I knows, and w'ot I seen I saw, and I 'ops it by the first train, and don't ask for no wages in loo of notice.

VAN HELSING: Where's Renfield?

ATTENDANT: If you asks me, I says 'e's probably payin' a little visit to 'ell.

SEWARD: You've let him escape again?

ATTENDANT: Look 'ere, sir. 'Avin', so to speak, resigned, I don't 'ave to put up with any more from any of you. [*Looks at* VAN HELSING *and* SEWARD.] W'ot a man can't 'elp, 'e can't 'elp, and that's that.

[SEWARD *sinks back on desk, head in hands.*]

VAN HELSING: Can't you see, man, that Doctor Seward is not well? Will you desert him when he needs all the help he can get?

ATTENDANT: Puttin' it that way, sir, I ain't the man to run under fire. But I'm sick and tired of being told off for what ain't my fault.

VAN HELSING: We don't blame you. No bolts or bars could hold Renfield.

Opposite: Frederick Pymm mesmerized Los Angeles audiences in a 1941 revival which also starred Dwight Frye, the original movie Renfield. (Courtesy of Ronald V. Borst/ Hollywood Movie Posters)

Bernard Jukes and Richard Coke in the 1939 London revival starring Hamilton Deane as Dracula. Shortly after this production, Jukes was killed in an air raid.

ATTENDANT: [SEWARD *looks up at him.*] Now, sir, you're talkin' sense. I 'ad 'im in a straitjacket this time. Nearly all yesterday I worked at clampin' bars across the winder. Now I finds them bars pulled apart like they was made o' cheese and 'im gone.

VAN HELSING: Then try to find him.

ATTENDANT: Find 'im, sir? Find 'im? I can't chase him up and down the wall. I ain't no bloody mountain goat! [*Exits.*]

VAN HELSING: The Thing mocks us. A few hours after he finds out what we know, and what we have done, he comes here, and drags that poor creature of his to himself.

SEWARD: [*In dull, hopeless tone.*] What can the vampire want with Renfield?

VAN HELSING: Renfield is serving an apprenticeship . . . to join the Vampire King after his death. We must prevent that.

SEWARD: What does Renfield matter? . . . If we are beaten, then there is no God.

VAN HELSING: [*Crosses to him.*] We dare not despair, Seward.

SEWARD: To figure out in advance what anyone would do who got on his track!

VAN HELSING: I thought we had him when we broke into Carfax and found two earth boxes there and then found one box in each of his four other houses, and when I pried up the lid of the sixth box I was sure we would find him there, helpless.

SEWARD: [*Bitterly.*] Empty.

VAN HELSING: An empty packing case, left as a blind.

SEWARD: He only brought six in his plane, so there can be only the one left.

VAN HELSING: Only one, but hidden where we can never find it. And now we've put him on his guard.

SEWARD: Yes. [*Chair turns back. Curtains flap out.* SEWARD *looks at wrist watch.*] It's not half an hour till sunrise. [*Rises and crossing to fireplace.*] Poor John has been sitting up with Lucy for nine hours. She'll be safe at dawn and he can get some sleep . . . if anyone can sleep in this house.

VAN HELSING: Whoever else sleeps or does not sleep, Miss Lucy will sleep at dawn.

SEWARD: Another horror?

VAN HELSING: Oh, you've noticed how she keeps awake all night now and sleeps by day.

SEWARD: Is that part of . . . the change?

VAN HELSING: Of course. And sometimes . . . the look that comes

Bela Lugosi puts the whammy on a summer-stock Van Helsing in the late 1940s. (Courtesy of Richard Bojarski)

into her face.

SEWARD: [*Turns face away in horror.*] Don't, man, for God's sake, I can't bear it!

VAN HELSING: We must face the facts, for her sake.

SEWARD: How could it have got at her with the wolfsbane and the cross around her neck? [*Pause.*] Suggestion, conveyed from the Monster?

VAN HELSING: Yes. He must have impelled the maid to take away the wolfsbane and cross and open the window. I should have foreseen that.

SEWARD: Don't blame yourself. The devil is more cunning than we are. [*Sits on couch.*] Yet Lucy seems better. Until this last attack she's always been exhausted, but at sunset last night, when she woke up after sleeping all day . . .

VAN HELSING: There was blood in her cheeks again.

SEWARD: Yes, thank God.

VAN HELSING: [*With terrible emphasis.*] My poor friend, *where does that blood come from?*

SEWARD: What do you suggest now? What fresh horror . . .

[*Door left opens a crack. Long skinny hand protrudes into room.* SEWARD *sees it first and starts in alarm. Rises.* VAN HELSING *turns quickly. Door opens slowly and* RENFIELD *slinks in.*]

RENFIELD: Is not half past five in the morning a strange hour for men who aren't crazy to be up and about? [*Crosses to window.*]

VAN HELSING: [*Aside to* SEWARD.] We may get help from this thing that's still half-human. [*To* RENFIELD.] Renfield.

RENFIELD: [*Crosses, with growing hysteria.*] He's after me! He's going to kill me!

VAN HELSING: Help us, Renfield, and we'll save you.

RENFIELD: You, you poor puny man, you measure your brains against his? You don't know what you're dealing with! You, a thick-headed Dutchman and a fool of an alienist, and a young cub of a boy. Why, not all the soldiers and police in London could stop the Master from doing as he likes.

VAN HELSING: But God can stop him!

Left to right: Stiano Braggiotti, Blanche Gladstone and Lowell Gilmore in a 1942 "subway circuit" production that entertained wartime audiences in Brooklyn and the Bronx. (Photofest)

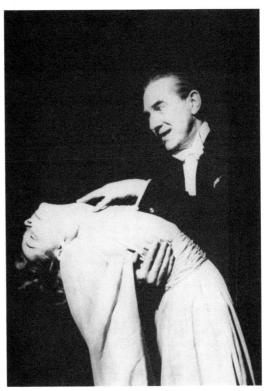

RENFIELD: God permits evil. Why does he permit evil if He is good?
  Tell me that.
SEWARD: How did you escape through those iron bars?
RENFIELD: [*Cunningly.*] Madmen have a great strength, Doctor.
VAN HELSING: Come, Renfield, we know you didn't wrench those bars
  apart yourself.
RENFIELD: [*Sane.*] No, I didn't. I wanted them there. I hoped they'd
  keep him out. He did it, then he called to me and I had to come.
  [*Back to insanity.*] The Master is angry. He promised me eternal
  life and live things, live things, big ones, not flies and spiders; and
  blood to drink, always blood. I must obey him but I don't want to
  be like him. . . . I am mad, I know, and bad, too, for I've taken
  lives, but they were only little lives. I'm not like him. I wouldn't
  like a human life. [LUCY *laughs offstage and says, "Oh, John!" as she*
  enters with HARKER. LUCY *has changed; there is blood in her cheeks, she*
  is stronger and seems full of vitality. She and HARKER *stop in surprise at*
  seeing RENFIELD. *To* LUCY.] And why did I seek to betray him? For

The seduction and the bite:
Bela Lugosi conquers Janet
Tyler in the 1943 revival. (The
Free Library of Philadelphia
Theatre Collection)

Van Helsing (Frank Jaquet) helps Lucy (Janet Tyler) break her addiction to Bela Lugosi in the 1943 revival tour. (The Free Library of Philadelphia Theatre Collection)

Wallace Widdecombe as Jonathan Harker attempts to rouse his Lucy (Janey Tyler) from her morbid reverie. From the 1943 revival. (The Free Library of Philadelphia Theatre Collection)

Opposite: A playbill for the 1943 Lugosi revival during its Philadelphia engagement. (The Free Library of Philadelphia Theatre Collection)

you. [*She smiles.*] I said I'd serve the devil, but I didn't serve him honestly. I don't like women with no blood in them. [LUCY *laughs.*] And yet I warned you and made him angry, and now . . . [*Working into frenzy.*] . . . perhaps he will kill me. [LUCY *laughs.*] And I won't get any more live things to eat. There'll be no more blood.

[RENFIELD *starts for* LUCY'*s throat.* HARKER *grasps him by right arm,* VAN HELSING *by left arm, then* SEWARD *steps in and takes* HARKER'*s place as* RENFIELD *struggles violently.* SEWARD *and* VAN HELSING *bear him away, struggling and screaming.*]

HARKER: Lucy, darling, you mustn't mind that poor, crazed creature.
LUCY: [*With low laugh as before.*] I don't. He amuses me.

[*She crosses to divan and sits.*]

HARKER: Oh, Lucy, how can you? The poor devil! Thank God . . . it will soon be dawn now.
LUCY: Dawn. The ebb tide of life. I hate the dawn. How can people like daylight? At night I am really alive. The night was made to enjoy life, and love. . . . [HARKER *turns to her; hesitates.*] Come to me, John, my own John.

[*He comes and sits next to her.*]

HARKER: Lucy, I'm so happy that you are better and strong again. . . .
LUCY: I've never been so well . . . so full of vitality. I was only a poor, washed-out, pale creature. I don't know what made you love me, John. There was no reason why you should. But there is *now.*
HARKER: I worship you.
LUCY: Then tell me something, John. [HARKER *turns slightly away.*] If you love me, you'll tell me. . . . Now don't turn away from me again.
HARKER: [*Wearily and sadly.*] You made me promise that I wouldn't tell you . . . anything.
LUCY: Oh, but I release you from your promise. There, now. What were you and Father and the funny Professor doing all day?
HARKER: I can't tell you. I promised.
LUCY: [*Angrily.*] You say you love me, but you don't trust me.
HARKER: I would trust you with my life, my soul.
LUCY: Then prove it. What were you doing . . . over there in Carfax? With the hammer and the horrible iron stake. [*He shakes his head. She registers anger. He puts his head in his hands, as though crying.*] You

The VAMPIRE PLAY!

FEW SHOWS IN THE ENTIRE HISTORY OF THE STAGE HOLD THE REAL THRILLS, EXCITEMENT AND BREATHTAKING SUSPENSE OF THIS WORLD FAMOUS HIT . . .

"SEE IT AND CREEP"—POST

"An Evening Rich in Horror"
—N. Y. TELEGRAM

"SHOULD BE SEEN BY ALL WHO LOVE THEIR MARROWS JOLTED"—N. Y. SUN

HARRY H. OSHRIN presents

Eminent Stage and Screen Star
IN PERSON

BELA
LUGOSI

in

DRACULA

Dramatized by Hamilton Deane and John L. Balderston
From Bram Stoker's Universally Renowned Novel
WITH A DISTINGUISHED BROADWAY CAST

"Nothing more blithely blood-curdling since 'The Bat'."—**N. Y. Herald Tribune**

"Sends shivers of apprehension streaming down the back." —**N. Y. Times**

LOCUST ST.
THEATRE
• PHILADELPHIA •

2 Weeks Only
BEG. MON. MAY 17

Eves.: 57c - $1.14 - $1.71 - $2.28 (Tax Inc.)
Mats. Thurs. and Sat. 57c - $1.14

don't think I'm asking you because . . . I'm just trying to find out whether you really love me. [HARKER *recoils from her, facing up.*] So you try to hide your schemes and your plots. Afraid I'd give them away, are you? You fools. Whatever *he* wants to know, he finds out for himself. He knows what you do. He knows what you think. He knows everything.

HARKER: Lucy!

> [*He puts his head in her lap and sobs.* LUCY *makes clawlike movement with both her hands, then as he sobs she changes attitude and gently strokes his head.*]

LUCY: My dear, I'm sorry. Let me kiss away the tears.

> [*She starts to kiss him. He quickly rises; backs away a few steps.*]

Ivan Butler and Hilda Campbell Russell perform the play's essential ritual in a British production of the late 1940s. (Courtesy of Ivan Butler)

HARKER: No, you mustn't kiss me! You made me promise not to let you kiss me.

LUCY: You don't know why I said that, John darling. It was because I love you so much. I was afraid of what might happen. You've always thought me cold, but I've blood in my veins, hot blood, my John. And I knew if I were to kiss you . . . but I'm not afraid now. Come, will you make me say it?

HARKER: Lucy, I don't understand you.

LUCY: [*Moves toward him.*] I love you. I want you. [*Stretches out her arms to him.*] Come to me, my darling. I want you.

HARKER: [*Goes to her, his resistance overcome, carried away by her ardor.*] Lucy, Lucy!

> [*He seizes her in his arms. Slowly she takes his head and bends it back. Slowly, triumphantly she bends her head down; her mouth hovers over his. Dogs howl outside. She bends his head further back quickly. Her mouth seeks his throat. Doors center open.* VAN HELSING *rushes in, holding crucifix.*]

John Carradine, one of the few actors who truly resembled Dracula as Stoker described him, makes a mesmeric pass at the maid in a 1950s revival. (Courtesy of Ronald V. Borst/Hollywood Movie Posters)

VAN HELSING: Harker! Harker, save yourself! [HARKER *rises, draws away. With outstretched arm,* VAN HELSING *holds crucifix between them.* LUCY's *face becomes convulsed with loathing and rage. She snarls like an animal, retreats, fainting onto divan.* VAN HELSING *follows, holds crucifix to her; strokes her forehead with left hand.*] I warned you, my poor friend. [*He kneels beside* LUCY; *begins to chafe her temples. She revives slowly, looks about her, sees cross and seizes it and kisses it passionately.* VAN HELSING, *fervently:*] Thank God! Thank God!

Lugosi gave his farewell stage performance of Dracula *in England in the early 1950s. (Courtesy of Ronald V. Borst/Hollywood Movie Posters)*

Like the Broadway *Dracula* that had preceded it fifty years earlier, the 1977 revival received decidedly mixed reviews that did nothing to slow the public's stampede to the box office. *The New York Times* critic Richard Eder declared the production "elegant," but "bloodless." "Mr. Langella is a stunning figure as Dracula," wrote Eder, "but he notably lacks terror." *Dracula*, in Eder's judgement, "comes to us with a stake through its heart, beyond real revival although capable of useful adornment."

Opposite: "The waxen face, the parted lips . . ." Frank Langella and Ann Sachs in the 1977 Broadway revival.

Frank Langella first played Dracula in a 1967 summer stock production in Stockbridge, Massachusetts. His co-star was Joanna Miles. (Courtesy of the Berkshire Theatre Festival)

[*Pause.* HARKER *crosses to divan.*]

LUCY: [*Broken-hearted.*] Don't come to me, John. I am unclean.

HARKER: [*Sits beside her.*] My darling, in my eyes you are purity itself.

VAN HELSING: You love her, and in love there is truth. She is pure, and the evil thing that has entered her shall be rooted out.

LUCY: [*In weak voice as in previous acts; to* VAN HELSING.] You said you could save Mina's soul.

VAN HELSING: Mina's soul is in heaven.

LUCY: [*Murmurs.*] Tell me how.

[SEWARD *enters, comes up to group in alarm, but* VAN HELSING *motions silence.*]

VAN HELSING: It is your right to know . . . now. I entered her tomb. I pried open the coffin. I found her there, sleeping, but not dead . . . not truly dead. There was blood in her cheeks, a drop of blood like a red ruby on the corner of her mouth. With a stake and hammer I struck to the heart. One scream, a convulsion, and then . . . the look of peace that came to her face when, with God's help, I had made her truly dead.

LUCY: If I die, swear to me that you will do this to my body.

VAN HELSING: It shall be done.

HARKER: I swear it.

SEWARD: And I.

LUCY: My lover, my father, my dear friend, you have sworn to save my soul. And now I am done with life. I cannot live on to become . . . what you know.

VAN HELSING: No, no, Miss Lucy, by all you hold sacred, you must not even think of suicide. That would put you in his power forever.

LUCY: I cannot face this horror that I am becoming.

HARKER: [*Rises.*] We will find this *Thing* that has fouled your life, destroy him and send his soul to burning hell, and it shall be by *my* hand.

LUCY: You must destroy him if you can, but with pity in your hearts, not rage and vengeance. That poor soul who has done so much evil needs our prayers more than any other. . . .

HARKER: No, you cannot ask me to forgive.

LUCY: Perhaps I, too, will need your prayers and your pity.

VAN HELSING: My dear Miss Lucy, now, while you are yourself, help me. [*Takes her hand.*]

LUCY: How can I help you? Don't tell me, no, you mustn't tell me anything.

Jean Le Clerc, soap-opera idol, brought cape-twirling French panache to the role.

Jeremy Brett, before his television success as Sherlock Holmes, made a credible Broadway Count.

Raul Julia was the first of many Langella replacements on Broadway. (Photofest)

VAN HELSING: Each time the white face, the red eyes came you were
   pale, exhausted afterwards. But that last time . . .

LUCY: [*Shudders.*] Last time he came he said I was his bride, he would
   seal me to him for the centuries to come.

VAN HELSING: And then?

LUCY: And then . . . [*Rises; crosses toward door.*] No, no, I can't tell
   you. I can't. . . .

VAN HELSING: But you must.

SEWARD: You must, Lucy!

LUCY: He scratched open one of his veins. He pressed my mouth
   down to it. He called it a mystic sacrament . . . he made me . . . he
   made me drink. . . . I can't, I can't . . . go on. . . . [LUCY *rushes off
   hysterically.* SEWARD *follows her.*]

VAN HELSING: I warned you, my poor friend. I broke in when I heard
   the dogs howling.

HARKER: The dogs. Then the Werewolf is about.

VAN HELSING: He is pursuing Renfield.

HARKER: God, we must do something!

VAN HELSING: And at once. I shall leave Renfield here, as I did Miss
   Lucy. If the *Thing* appears, we three will bar the two doors and the
   window.

HARKER: [*Crosses up toward window. Laughs bitterly.*] Bar? Against
   that?

VAN HELSING: Even against *that,* for we shall each carry the sacred
   element.

HARKER: And then?

VAN HELSING: Then I do not know. It will be terrible, for we do not
   know his full powers. But this I know. . . . [*Looks at watch.*] It is
   eight minutes to sunrise. The power of all evil things ceases with
   the coming of day. His one last earth box is his only refuge. If we
   can keep him here till daybreak he must collapse. And the stake
   and the hammer are ready. [*Dogs howl.* HARKER *crosses to window,
   goes out.*] He is here. Quickly! [VAN HELSING *runs to window. Seizes
   RENFIELD.*]

RENFIELD: [*As he is dragged in by* VAN HELSING.] No, no!

VAN HELSING: But you must, man, and this may save your soul and
   your life as well.

RENFIELD: No, no, no, not alone! Don't leave me alone! [VAN
   HELSING *shoves him forward.* RENFIELD *falls.* VAN HELSING *hurries
   out, closing door and putting lights out.* RENFIELD *slowly rises; looks
   about him.* RENFIELD *howls in terror; crouches in firelight as far away as*

*Terence Stamp took the title
role in the 1978 London production of the Edward Gorey
revival. Unlike the American
success, however, the British engagement performed dismally.*

Walter Kerr, writing in the Sunday *New York Times*, best described the effect of Edward Gorey's sets and costumes: "The curtain rises not on a room but on a cartoon, a massive two-dimensional pen-and-ink sketch carrying us upward like a beehive tomb at Mycenae; and everywhere in its intricate strokes lurk the outline of bats' wings: bats' wings worked into the fireplace mantle, bats' wings worked into the cornices and pediments, bats' wings worked into the upholstered blue-gray furniture. When heroine Lucy comes on, dancing to an ancient radio and sipping from the blood-red contents of her wineglass, we discover—as she extends her arms—that her gown drapes into bats' wings, too."

Opposite: David Dukes filled the Edward Gorey sets with an additional air of menace. (Photofest)

Despite the uniform critical praise for his set designs, Edward Gorey—amazingly—disliked the production. "I tend not to like any of my work, and this production least of all," he told the *New York Post.* "It wasn't a labor of love. I did it purely for the money."

possible from doors and window. DRACULA *appears, door center, in pale blue light, in evening clothes, dress and cloak as before. Red light from fireplace covers* DRACULA. *As* DRACULA *moves,* RENFIELD'*s back is to audience.*] Master! I didn't do it! I said nothing. I am your slave, your dog! [DRACULA *steps toward him.*] Master, don't kill me! For the love of God, let me live. Punish me . . . torture me . . . I deserve it . . . but let me live! I can't face God with all those lives on my conscience, all that blood on my hands.

DRACULA: [*With deadly calm.*] Did I not promise you that you should come to me at your death, and enjoy centuries of life and power over the bodies and souls of others?

RENFIELD: Yes, Master, I want lives, I want blood . . . but I didn't want human life.

DRACULA: You betrayed me. You sought to warn my destined bride against me.

RENFIELD: Mercy, mercy, mercy, don't kill me!

[DRACULA *raises right arm very slowly toward* RENFIELD, *who screams, this time in physical pain.* RENFIELD, *like a bird before a snake, drags himself to* DRACULA, *who stands motionless. As* RENFIELD *reaches* DRACULA'*s feet,* DRACULA, *with swift motion, stoops, seizes him by the throat, lifts him up, his grip stifling* RENFIELD'*s screams. Doors center are thrown open.* VAN HELSING *switches on lights.* DRACULA *drops* RENFIELD, *who falls into corner below couch and remains there during following scene.* DRACULA *starts toward* VAN HELSING, *who takes case containing Host out of inside breast pocket and holds it out toward* DRACULA *in his clenched right fist.* DRACULA *recoils; turns quickly to window.* HARKER *appears through window and holds crucifix toward* DRACULA *in clenched fist.* DRACULA *recoils.* SEWARD *enters window, holding crucifix. The three men stand during the following scene with right arms pointing toward* DRACULA. *He turns, walks to fireplace, turns and faces them.*]

DRACULA: [*Ironically.*] My friends, I regret I was not present to receive your calls at my house.

VAN HELSING: [*Looks at watch.*] Four minutes until sunrise.

DRACULA: [*Looking at wrist watch.*] Your watch is correct, Professor.

VAN HELSING: Your life in death has reached its end.

SEWARD: By God's mercy.

DRACULA: [HARKER *steps toward* DRACULA. DRACULA, *turning to them,*

The flying bats in the 1977
production of *Dracula* involved considerably more
technical derring-do than
the fishing-pole flappers
employed by Hamilton De-
ane. Technician Tim Abel
spent each performance sus-
pended thirty-eight feet
above the stage on a special
platform, outfitted with a
safety harness that let him
lean forward like a pup-
peteer to manipulate the
flight trajectories of the
black-winged beasties on
their appointed rounds.
One bat was used ex-
clusively for the curtain
call, and on holidays Abel
would outfit the creature
with appropriate costume
pieces—Easter Bunny ears,
a Santa Claus beard,
Fourth of July flags, and
so on.

suavely.] Its end? Not yet, Professor. I have still more than three minutes to add to my five hundred years.

HARKER: And three minutes from now you'll be in hell, where a thousand years of agony will not bring you one second nearer the end of your punishment.

VAN HELSING: Silence, Harker. Miss Lucy forbade this. She asked for prayer, and for pity. [*To* DRACULA.] Make your peace with God, Man-That-Was. We are not your judges . . . we know not how this curse may have come upon you.

DRACULA: [*Furiously.*] You fools! You think with your wafers, your wolfsbane, you can destroy me . . . me, the king of my kind? You shall see. Five of my earth boxes you have polluted. Have you found the sixth?

VAN HELSING: You cannot reach your sixth refuge now. Take your true form as Werewolf if you will. Your fangs may rend us, but we have each sworn to keep you here . . . [*Looks at watch.*] . . . for two minutes and a half, when you must collapse and we can make an end.

DRACULA: *You* keep *me.* Fools, listen and let my words ring in your ears all your lives, and torture you on your deathbeds! I go, I go to sleep in my box for a hundred years. You have accomplished that much against me, Van Helsing. But in a century I shall wake, and call my bride to my side from her tomb, my Lucy, my Queen. [HARKER *and* SEWARD *move closer.*] I have other brides of old times who await me in their vaults in Transylvania. But I shall set *her* above them all.

HARKER: Should you escape, we know how to save Lucy's soul, if not her life.

DRACULA: [*Moving left.*] Ah, the stake. Yes, but only if she dies by day. I shall see that she dies by night. She shall come to an earth box of mine at her death and await her Master. To do to her what you did to my Mina, Van Helsing, you must find her body, and that you will not.

HARKER: Then she shall die by day.

DRACULA: You will kill her? You lack the courage, you poor rat of flesh and blood!

SEWARD: Silence, John . . . he is doomed. This is his revenge. He hopes to trouble us . . . afterwards.

VAN HELSING: [*Looks at watch.*] Thirty seconds.

[*They move in.*]

*Like Lugosi, Frank Langella
followed his Broadway success
in Dracula with a film version
for Universal in 1979.*

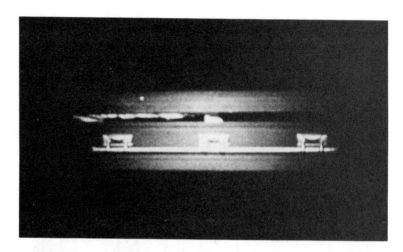

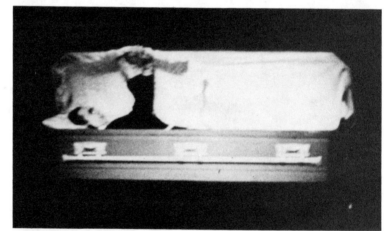

Lugosi often incorporated scenes from Dracula *for vaudeville engagements. Here, he makes his inimitable entrance in a post-war stage show. (Courtesy of Richard Bojarski)*

DRACULA: [*Calmly, suavely again.*] I thank you for reminding me of the time.

VAN HELSING: Harker, open the curtains. [HARKER *opens curtains. Red light of approaching dawn outside.*] That is the East. The sun will rise beyond the meadow there.

[DRACULA *pulls cape over his head.*]

SEWARD: [*Glancing behind, leaves wolfsbane on desk as he looks up at window.*] The clouds are coloring.

HARKER: God's daybreak.

[HARKER *leaves crucifix on desk.* VAN HELSING *checks watch.* SEWARD *and* HARKER *step in.*]

DRACULA: [*Coolly. Turns upstage, with back to them.*] A pleasant task you have set yourself, Mr. Harker.

VAN HELSING: Ten seconds. Be ready when he collapses.

[SEWARD *crosses to hold* DRACULA'*s cape on left of* DRACULA. HARKER *holds cape on right of* DRACULA.]

HARKER: *The sun!* The stake, Professor . . . the stake! Hold him, Doctor.

SEWARD: I've got him.

[DRACULA, *with loud burst of mocking laughter, vanishes on the word "sun," leaving the two men holding the empty cape. A flash goes off in front of fireplace.* HARKER *backs down left, drops empty cape in front of desk. The three men look around them.*]

HARKER: Up the chimney, as a bat. You heard what he said?

SEWARD: God will not permit it. What's to be done now, Van Helsing?

VAN HELSING: [*Crosses, after looking at the prostrate* RENFIELD; *motions* HARKER *and* SEWARD *to him. Whispers to them.*] We'll trick Renfield into showing us! [*Then:*] Dare we leave Renfield on earth to become the slave when he dies?

SEWARD: But he's human. We can't do murder?

HARKER: I'll do it if you won't, Doctor!

VAN HELSING: [*To* SEWARD.] Go to your office and get some painless drug.

RENFIELD: [*Sensing their drift without hearing their words, has been edging toward panel. Looks around room, then at panel.*] They're going to kill

In Liveright's Broadway production, Dracula's disappearance was accomplished in plain view of the audience with the aid of a hydraulic trap door set into the library carpet. Lugosi wore a cape long enough to cover his heels and with a collar large enough to cover the back of his head. The shoulders of the cape were reinforced with wire to allow the actor to slip down the trap unnoticed. A flash-bomb in the fireplace distracted the audience as the trap door moved back into place, leaving the other actors holding the empty cloak. (The illusion revived an old stage trick—the "vampire trap" was first introduced in James Robinson Planché's *The Vampire, or, The Bride of the Isles* in 1820.) For Liveright's subsequent touring productions of *Dracula*, the technical difficulties were avoided through the use of a simple blackout or blinding flash while Dracula made his exit through a wall panel.

me, Master! Save me! I am coming to you.

[*Panel in bookcase opens,* RENFIELD *exits and panel closes.*]

VAN HELSING: He has shown us the way! Where does that passage go?
SEWARD: I never knew there was a passage.

[HARKER *hastens to desk; gets stake and hammer. They rush to panel.*]

VAN HELSING: Only that devil has the combination. We'll break through somehow. Harker ... quick, the hammer.

BLACKOUT

CURTAIN

The final curtain: Bela Lugosi went to his grave in 1956, resplendent in Dracula costume and makeup. Below: a souvenir packet of earth from Lugosi's grave, sold by mail-order to the morbidly curious in the early 1990s. (Courtesy of Jeanne Youngson)

SCENE 2

A vault.

Absolute darkness. Coffin right center and back of gauze drop. Flash of electric torch seen coming slowly downstairs center. Coffin contains body of DRACULA.

VAN HELSING'S VOICE: For God's sake, be careful, Seward.
SEWARD'S VOICE: These stairs go down forever.
VAN HELSING'S VOICE: May God protect us.
SEWARD'S VOICE: Is Harker there?
VAN HELSING'S VOICE: He's gone for a lantern.
SEWARD'S VOICE: I've got to the bottom.
VAN HELSING'S VOICE: Be careful. I'm right behind you.

[*Torch flashes around vault and they walk about slowly.*]

SEWARD'S VOICE: What can this place be?
VAN HELSING'S VOICE: It seems an old vault. [*Stifled scream from* SEWARD. *Torch out. The torch is seen to jerk back.*] What is it? Oh, where are you, man?
SEWARD'S VOICE: Sorry. I'm all right. A big rat ran across my foot.

[*Light seen coming downstairs.* HARKER *appears carrying lighted lantern which reaches floor; partially illuminates bare vault. He has stake and hammer in left hand.*]

HARKER: Where are you? What is this place?   *"Let me drive it in deep!"*
VAN HELSING: We can't see.

[HARKER *moves with lantern.*]

HARKER: The place smells horribly of bats.
VAN HELSING: It has an animal smell, like the lair of a wolf.
HARKER: That's what it is.
SEWARD: [*Still flashing torch about.*] There's absolutely nothing here.
HARKER: [*At extreme left with lantern.*] Here's another passage.
VAN HELSING: [*Moving left.*] I thought so. That must lead to Carfax.
The sixth earth box is hidden somewhere here.
HARKER: And the monster is in it.
SEWARD: You can't be sure. [*As he speaks, light from his torch falls on*
RENFIELD, *stretched on floor.* RENFIELD *screams as light falls on him;*
scurries off right into darkness.] Renfield!

[HARKER *and* VAN HELSING *hurry across.*]

VAN HELSING: Where is he?
SEWARD: Over there somewhere. Even if Renfield knew about this

For the Broadway production, Liveright toned down Dracula's demise considerably, and at first eliminated Hamilton Deane's trick box and crumbling body; Dracula, deep in his box, was invisible to the audience. Brooks Atkinson noted the odd restraint: ". . . they kill him with one blow on a stake sent through his heart. Several additional blows, given with a hearty grunt or two would seem a good deal more conclusive: Count Dracula deserves a steam hammer." Late in the play's run, Liveright added a Deane-style coffin trick, generating added publicity.

Van Helsing's curtain speech was filmed as a tongue-in-cheek epilogue for Universal's film version of *Dracula* and appeared in all prints for the film's initial release in 1931. The sequence was deleted when the film was re-released in 1938 for fear that the joke would be taken literally by church groups as an endorsement of vampire beliefs.

place, that doesn't prove the vampire's here.

VAN HELSING: [*As* SEWARD *is speaking* VAN HELSING *moves right; seizes* RENFIELD.] It is the vampire's life or yours! [*Drags* RENFIELD *into light of lantern.*] Look at him, man, look at him. He knows.

RENFIELD: I know nothing. Let me go! Let me go, I say! [*Breaks away; goes right.*]

VAN HELSING: He was stretched out here, but he wouldn't let me drag him back. Ah! Here it is. Quick, that stake.

[HARKER *and* VAN HELSING, *with stake, pry up stone slab and open coffin. The three men gaze in horror and triumph at coffin.*]

SEWARD: What a horrible undead thing he is lying there!

HARKER: Let me drive it in deep!

[VAN HELSING *takes stake from* HARKER, *lowers it into the coffin.* RENFIELD *stands at right end of coffin.*]

VAN HELSING: [*Almost in a whisper.*] That's over the heart, Doctor?

SEWARD: [*Back of coffin.*] Yes. [VAN HELSING *hands hammer to* HARKER. HARKER *raises hammer high over head; pounds stake with full force. Low groan. Silence. Stake remains fixed in* DRACULA's *body.*]

VAN HELSING: See his face now . . . the look of peace.

SEWARD: He is crumbling away.

RENFIELD: Thank God, we're free!

LUCY: [*Comes down stairway and halts at bottom.*] Father, Father, John!

HARKER: Lucy!

VAN HELSING: [*Takes handful of dust; scatters it over the body.*] Dust to dust . . . ashes to ashes . . .

CURTAIN

[*The curtain rises again and the entire cast comes downstage before a black drop for curtain speech.*]

VAN HELSING: [*To* AUDIENCE.] Just a moment, Ladies and Gentlemen! Just a word before you go. We hope the memories of Dracula and Renfield won't give you bad dreams, so just a word of reassurance. When you get home tonight and the lights have been turned out and you are afraid to look behind the curtains and you dread to see a face appear at the window . . . why, just pull yourself together and remember that after all *there are such things.*

THE CURTAIN FALLS

Edward Van Sloan delivers the play's tongue-in-cheek curtain speech in a scene now lost from the 1931 film version.

Acknowledgments

The editor gratefully acknowledges the many people and institutions who helped make this book possible. Robert A. Freedman of the Robert A. Freedman Dramatic Agency, Inc., provided the essential contact with the Deane and Balderston estates, now represented by John Balderston and Ann Burton (additional thanks to agent Laurence Fitch in London). My own agent, Malaga Baldi, brought the book to the attention of St. Martin's Press, where editor Gordon Van Gelder enthusiastically recognized the project's potential.

Services, courtesies, suggestions and other valuable forms of support were provided by John Allen, Richard Bojarski, Ronald V. Borst, Bernard Davies, Geraldine Duclow, Joe Marc Freedman, Galowitz Photographics, Inc., Donal F. Holway, Robert James Leake, Loraine Machlin, Ron and Howard Mandelbaum at Photofest, Scott MacQueen, William G. Obbagy, Garydon Rhodes, Scott Wolfman, and Jeanne Youngson.

Institutional collections consulted included the Bobst Library of New York University, British Library Division of Manuscripts, the New York Public Library (especially the Billy Rose Theatre Collection at Lincoln Center), the Free Library of Philadelphia Theatre Collection, the Harvard Theatre Collection, the Margaret Herrick Library of the Academy of Motion Picture Arts and Sciences, the Library of Congress, the Theatre Museum, and the collections of the Dracula Society in London and the Count Dracula Fan Club in New York.

A final acknowledgement is reserved for all the readers of *Hollywood Gothic* who, like me, just couldn't get enough Dracula. You know who you are, and this book is for you.